CRUCIBLE OF A NEW NATION

FIRST YORK COUNTY COURT HOUSE
1754   1841

by

HELEN MILLER GOTWALT

Research Consultant   *Landon Charles Reisinger*
Artist   *James Rudisill*

Published and Copyrighted 1977 by York County Bicentennial Commission, Inc.
John F. Rauhauser, Jr., Pres.

Acknowledgments

This publication has been made possible through the cooperation and assistance of numerous individuals, organizations and business enterprises. But those primarily and most directly responsible, to whom the York County Bicentennial Commission extends its very sincere thanks, on behalf of the York County Community are: Publication Committee, Melvin Campbell, Chairman* , Helen Miller Gotwalt, James Rudisill, and Landon Charles Reisinger for their arduous efforts in research, writing, preparation of cover and illustrative materials and all those other rewarding and unrewarding tasks involved in the publication of this volume.

American Revolution Bicentennial Administration, for original funding, by a matching fund grant.

Bicentennial Commission of Pennsylvania, for the application to the American Revolution Bicentennial Administration, on behalf of the York County Bicentennial Commission, the processing and the administration of the grant.

The York Bank and Trust Company, York's first and oldest bank, for its generosity in providing the local matching funds for this project.

The P.H. Glatfelter Co., for donating the excellent, quality paper upon which this book is published.

The Anstadt Company and its personnel, for its interest and attention to detail beyond its basic printing assignment.

The Martin Memorial Library Reference Staff for their many services.

The Historical Society of York County for records and graphics.

* Deceased

A special and particular debt of gratitude is due to a very special community servant of York County, — Helen Miller Gotwalt, who authored this book. Her research and study in preparation for writing this book, her dedicated devotion to the assignment, her imaginative use of the materials, her persuasive and diplomatic requests for assistance, together with yet another exhibition of her exceptional talent as a writer and story teller, — all demonstrate once again the best elements of professionalism and citizenship, generally, — and, the beautiful character of Helen Miller Gotwalt, in particular.

Her product on these pages is unique. But then, so is she.

To Sam Gotwalt, her husband, for his patience and tolerance, as well as for his thoughtful and helpful suggestions we also extend our thanks.

Preface

One of the finer qualities of human nature is a veneration for the past by scholastic interest or sentimental attachment for the heritage which made us what we are today.

In the darkest hours of the Revolution the little Court House in York, Pennsylvania served as the meeting place for representatives of the thirteen colonies — a haven and refuge from pursuing British forces. For nine months its walls echoed the debates of Continental Congress over conflicting interests and manifold problems which culminated in the adoption of the Articles of Confederation — the first Constitution of the United States.

Demolished in 1841, this cornerstone of constitutional government existed only in deeds and documents, in archives and archetypes, until, under the dedicated and inspirational leadership of Attorney John F. Rauhauser, Jr., the York County Bicentennial Commission erected an accurate, full scale replica of the sacred structure in downtown York.

As a "Heritage Gift to the Nation", the reconstructed Court House has created a new understanding and awareness of York's unique role in American history. For the Court House at York Town was, indeed, the CRUCIBLE in which the molten metal of a new nation was formed and tested during the bleak winter of 1777-1778. It was here that thirteen independent colonies were fused into a confederacy stiled by its founders THE UNITED STATES OF AMERICA.

The story of the First York County Court House is the story of a town and its people, the story of a county and its conflicts, the story of a country and its capitol. Published in commemoration of the 200th anniversary of the adoption of the Articles of Confederation by Continental Congress, November 15, 1777, THE CRUCIBLE OF A NEW NATION is a biography of the building where the United States began. May it serve to edify us and our posterity on the origin of the finest system of government conceived in the mind of the human race.

Richard E. Kohler
President Judge, Orphans' Court
Division, Court of Common Pleas
York County, Pennsylvania

Table of Contents

THE CRUCIBLE

First York County Court House as reconstructed by
York County Bicentennial Commission, Inc. 1976

A Building Speaks

The People Listen

1

There can be no question that historic buildings speak to those who know how to listen. Their voices are not silenced by time, and many speak in louder, clearer accents long after their walls have crumbled, their timbers vanished, and their foundations buried beneath the paving stones of Progress. This is the story of one such building.

The reconstruction of York County's Provincial Court House, dedicated May 1st, 1976 as the heritage gift of York Countians to the nation in the Bicentennial Era, was accomplished by those who had learned to listen and to interpret what they heard. For eighty five years, from its completion in 1756 until its demolition in 1841, the original building in the Court House Square, constructed by order of the General Assembly of the Province of Pennsylvania was the oracle of the law, the voice of Justice, and the articulation of government.

At the onset of the Revolution the building stones vibrated to fifes and drums, cheering crowds, the tramp of marching feet, as the first York Volunteers went off to war. In 1776 the York Liberty Bell rang in the new age of Independence from the Court House Square. The following year, with the arrival of a hard-pressed Congress fleeing British-occupied Philadelphia, the crowded court room echoed the decisions of distraught but determined delegates struggling, behind closed doors, to bring together the divergent views of thirteen newly independent colonies; to compromise their conflicts of interest and unite them, under law, for "common defense, the security of . . . liberty and . . . mutual and general welfare . . ."

"The spacious times . . .
with sounds that echo still."
Tennyson

1

On November 15, 1777 this struggle culminated in the adoption of The Articles of Confederation, the first of which established that "The Stile of this Confederacy shall be 'THE UNITED STATES OF AMERICA.'"

A new nation had been born within the whitewashed walls of the little court house at York Town.

Thirteen separate colonies were forged into a single nation with a constitutional government empowered to handle affairs at home and abroad, thereby winning recognition in Europe, and expediting the French Alliance so desperately needed to turn defeat into victory. And so, the two storied structure which housed the sole governing body of this newly formed nation, the structure in which all affairs of state were conducted until June 28, 1778, was no longer a provincial court house, but rather The National Capitol, in the Town of York, Pennsylvania, which, on the same basis, lays just and lasting claim to the title — FIRST CAPITAL OF THE UNITED STATES.

But so fleeting is fame, and so rapid the pace of time and change, that sixty three years later the demands of growth and progress forced the demolition of this historic structure and adjacent Office Building in favor of new and larger court accommodations. The very doors and windows must have rattled in protest. And there were those who listened. One irate citizen voiced his sentiments in THE REPUBLICAN dated Wednesday, June 23, 1841.

The Court House

An advertisement in this and the other papers of the county announces the intention of the Commissioners to offer the Old Court House at Public Sale in the early part of next month. The disposition to be made of the building afterwards will, we suppose, be left to the determination of the purchaser, though we may take it for granted that the conditions of sale will require it to be removed from its present site. We plead guilty to a feeling which it would be too strong certainly to call reverence, and smack too much of mercenary motive to style interest, for the venerable structure. This arises, not from its "outward adornment", for certainly it has no pretensions to architectural beauty; but, although our blood is somewhat more cold than of yore, and we are not so impressible as then on such subjects, we are actuated in this matter by a regard for the associations which cluster around the old building. If its exterior be plain, rough, and, worst of all in these days, UNFASHIONABLE, its interior is hallowed by remembrance that there sat the pure patriots, the wise statesmen and moral heroes of a better age in solemn council and "high debate" — the pilots of that freedom-Freighted barque which was struggling amid the boiling waves of war to attain the safe harbor of liberty and independence. All our aspirations in this behalf go out for the preservation of the old Court House, for though the cynical may sneer and the miserly may frown, we hold it good to preserve all the memorials — the substantial and tangible mementoes of the Revolution, in order to fan the flame that too often slumbers of a disinterested love of country. We do not wish to be mis- understood; it may be unadvisable to continue the building in its present situation, and it may be impossible to remove it; we undertake to judge of neither. What we would say is, that as a Town Hall for the holding of public meetings and transactions of various kinds of business is much needed in our Borough, we would rejoice to see the old Court House, if it could be removed, purchased by the Burgesses, placed on some eligible spot of ground, and repaired and fitted up in such a manner as would at once conduce to public accommodation & the preservation of the ancient and hallowed building in our midst. This is all that we have to say on this point, and we submit it to the consideration of our good citizens.

But the "good citizens" were not good listeners. No one came to the rescue and THE REPUBLICAN for September 15, 1841 published what might well have been entitled

REQUIEM FOR THE OLD COURT HOUSE

The relic of an ante-revolutionary period, which was hallowed as having been the Council-Hall of the Continental Congress in the darkest days of the struggle for Freedom, is now rapidly disappearing under the ruthless hand of modern improvement. Those ancient walls in which rung the appeals of Patriotism, and where Justice steadied her scales amid the ratio- cination and eloquence — "the wisdom and the wit" — the sharp sarcasm and "the tart reply," are being rapidly levelled with the ground. We can- not but recall at this time the remark of a distinguished citizen, the Hon. John C. Wright, of Ohio, who when passing through our Borough a short time ago and learning that it was intended to pull down the ancient building, said that not one brick should be touched, nor should the structure be removed one inch from its present site, had he the power, for the time would come when pilgrimages would be made to those buildings so intimately associated with the toils and triumphs of the Revolution — that they would become the Meccas of Freedom, where her sons would congregate to rekindle in their bosoms the sacred flame of gratitude to the deliverers of their country and of devotion to those principles which they

3

had defended. But the Old Court House is gone — and who shall record its history, marked by many interesting incidents during the century through which it stood, or write the lives of the men yet unknown to fame who were identified with it in their labors and exertions..........................

Arms of the state of Pennsylvania painted in 1796 by John Fisher for the first York County Courthouse.

But even though the Old Court House was so wantonly destroyed, there were some valuable survivals. The foundation stones were still in place; the Pennsylvania Coat of Arms painted in oil on panel by John Fisher in 1796, was re-hung in the new court house; the wooden statue of Justice carved by the same hand in the same year was salvaged by one of the carpenters; another Fisher creation, the Pulaski weathervane was rescued from the rubble by members of the Laurel Fire Company; various pieces of furniture were purchased at public sale and handed down from one generation to another; and, beyond all price, the Court Records, the County Commissioners' Minute Books and Treasurers' reports were carefully preserved.

"A time to gather stones together"
Ecclesiastes

In 1841 no one could have guessed that in another century this fallen structure would rise again, in a new location, not by some miracle as the fabled Phoenix rose from its own ashes, but completely and faithfully re-created, and painstakingly assembled by human hands, from these existing relics and records.

The idea was not new. On April 28, 1930 York Congressman Franklin Menges introduced a resolution requesting a congressional appropriation of $300,000 "to be expended by the federal government for the purpose of designing and constructing a memorial building in York, Pennsylvania, at or near the site where the Continental Congress held its sessions from September 30, 1777 to June 28, 1778. But 1930 was not a good year. The country, still shaken by the stock market crash of Black Tuesday in 1929, was on the verge of the Great Depression. There were no federal funds available to "commemorate York's part in the American Revolution." The resolution was rejected.

However, in the more favorable climate of the Bicentennial Era, the plan to reconstruct this "Shrine of Freedom" received local, state and Federal support. "Greater than the tread of mighty armies", wrote Victor Hugo, "is an idea whose time has come." The time for rebuilding the Court House that became a Capitol had definitely arrived. In selecting this project, the York County Bicentennial Commission fulfilled the basic intent and purpose of "America's Birthday." It honored York's heritage with something of permanence, of utility, and of educational value; it created something to be used and enjoyed by York Countians, visitors and tourists; it focused attention on York's great history, too long neglected; it contributed to York's pride, revitalization, beauty and culture; and, finally, it realized a hope and dream of the York County Community, expressed

"A time to build up"
Ecclesiastes

5

frequently and in many ways since the original building was demolished in 1841.

Since the historic court house could not possibly be reconstructed at its original location in the middle of Continental Square, the York County Bicentennial Commission was faced with the problem of acquiring a suitable building site. The eventual choice was a 200' x 200' tract at the North West corner of Market Street and Pershing Avenue.

Few, if any of the spectators who attended the Ground-Breaking Ceremony on the rainy afternoon of September 1, 1975, were aware of the historical significance of this property which extends westward from Pershing Avenue along the north side of Market Street as far as the Codorus Creek. But its original ownership dates back to the very founding of this "Second City of the Penns."

As early as 1690 William Penn had proposed a new settlement on the Susquehanna, but his dream was not realized until more than a score of years after his death, when two German settlers literally "came out of the wilderness" to approach his son Thomas with a plan for establishing a town at the intersection of the Monocacy Road and the Codorus Creek.

One of these men was Baltzer Spangler who later recounted how he and "a certain Ulrick Wisler, then his neighbor, in the deep snow, in the year 1739 or 1740, Traveld to Philadelphia, and waited on the Honorable Thomas Penn Esqr., and inform'd him of a Piece of Land suitable to build a Town on, which then lay vacant, and Adjoining the Land Granted him by the Said Proprietor in the year 1736; and Requested the Proprietor, that he should be pleas'd to order a Town to be Laid out, on the said Piece of Land, for Tradesmen &ca."

Spangler further related how in the "Fall following", Thomas Cookson came to his house with a letter from the Proprietor the contents of which were that he and Wisler show Mr. Cookson the land they had mentioned; that, if it was indeed a suitable place for a Town, they would assist him in laying it out, and, that in reward for their services, each of them should have a lot of his own choosing.

According to these terms, when they had fulfilled their part of the bargain, Cookson "laid out to Ulrick Wisler a lot in High Street Adjoining the Creek, which he afterwards sold" and to Spangler "a lot on the Corner of the Square, which is known on the General Plan of the town by the Number 70."

From this account and from further research pinpointing Wisler's lot

on the north side of West Market Street, it is evident that the 1976 Court House occupies one of the first two holdings in York Town.

On Historic Ground

The Plan of York as Laid Out by Thomas Cookson (1741) and George Stevenson (1754) shows this same lot, listed as #326, to have been owned in 1765 by the Quaker shopkeeper, Nathan Hussey. Hussey was one of the committee designated by the Provincial Assembly to acquire the original Court House site in 1749.

Lot #124, diagonally across the street, was first issued to George Swope, also a member of that committee, and was later assigned to John Meem, one of the carpenters for the original construction. In 1741, Martin Eichelberger, a German innkeeper, procured Lot #120, due East of the court house, on which he built the now famous Golden Plough Tavern used by farmers and travelers until 1850, and restored in 1963 as an architectural landmark. In Revolutionary times, the dwelling on the south west corner of the intersection was the residence of Captain Michael Doudel, who led the first York County troops to the relief of General Washington in 1775.

These historic associations, which so firmly link the present with the past, also serve to confirm the court house, not merely as a monument to, but as an interpreter of York's colonial heritage.

Integrity of Design

From the outset, the Bicentennial planners were pledged to the idea that the new building would be an authentic reproduction — an honest, and, in so far as possible, an exact replica of the First Capitol. The obvious starting point, therefore, would have been the original building plans. But those plans had long since been lost or destroyed. Existing prints and sketches, although rich in architectural detail, portray the court house as it looked after the renovations of 1796 and 1814-15, not as it was first constructed and used by Continental Congress in 1777-78.

Lacking both plans and pictures, it was, therefore, necessary to examine documents, peruse petitions, study specifications, scrutinize agreements and correspondence, check out expenditures, and research every available source of information pertaining to the original design, construction and furnishing. If the reconstruction was to be more than a superficial "look-alike", the 18th century records must become the 20th century blueprints.

The Minute Books of the York County Commissioners for 1754-56 proved to be a veritable construction manual. The Commissioners themselves, acting as the building contractors, entered into separate agreements with individual workmen as "sub-contractors" for labor and materials.

From these Articles of Agreement, which explicitly defined the specifications for every phase of construction, the present-day builders set up their architectural guide-lines.

Labor and Materials

The first such Article of Agreement, January 31, 1754, between the Commissioners, Bartholomew Maul, John Mickell, and James Agnew, of the one part, and William Willis, bricklayer, of the other, illustrates this point.

> *"First That said William Willis shall make or cause to be made a quantity of good hard bricks sufficient to build a Court House of such dimensions as shall be hereafter agreed of by the said Commissioners, each brick when well burnt, to be nine inches in length, four inches and one quarter in breadth and two inches and one quarter thick, to be made of clay dug before the date hereof."*

Thus it was by design rather than by accident that the bricks used in the new Court House were made to these exact specifications, their color carefully chosen to match, as closely as possible, a few existing samples.

A further study of the Willis agreement designated the depth of the stone foundation as two feet below the ground (or deeper, depending upon conditions) and two feet above the ground . . . another authentic piece of the architectural puzzle.

Those early County Commissioners knew exactly what they wanted and, with characteristic German thoroughness and English tenacity, made sure they would get it. Nothing was left to chance. There were carefully worded, precise agreements with Henry Clark of Warrington Township for scantlings and lumber including 1,000 feet of "good seasoned inch poplar boards" and a similar amount of "good oak boards; with Joseph Welschance to make all the smith work . . . straps, bolts and cramping the roof" . . . hooks, hinges and fastenings . . . even "the spier at the top of the turret which he will do as cheap as it can be afforded:" with Joseph Heald for "good clean sand;" with Anna Mary and Christopher Dottenheffer "six hundred bushels of good unslaked lime:"; and with Robert Jones "to bring 7,000 cedar shingles from Philadelphia."

But the agreement which most influenced the appearance of the building was that of March 7, 1754 with John Meem and Jacob Kline "to do all the Carpenters' and Joiners' work. Under the terms of this contract, they agreed "to make a large neat and plain door case with a pair of folding doors, containing 8 panels of good neat quarter round work and to line the said doors and hang the same . . . to make 17 sash window cases suitable for

8

sashes to contain 24 panes of glass ten by twelve inches square...to make 17 pairs of shutters containing six panels and line same, and hang the said shutters to the windows and fix the fastening to the same.''

This agreement also provided for ''a cupola or turret nearly like that on the Court House in the Borough of Lancaster.''

Slowly, but authentically, a word picture was taking shape. However, there was one important question these records failed to answer: What were the actual dimensions of the Court House? William Willis had been directed to ''make build or erect the walls of a court house on such ground as the said Commissioners lay out and show him for that purpose near the center of the town of York in the County aforesaid and of such dimension as shall be hereafter agreed on.......in sufficient workman-like manner, agreeable to a plan of said court house to be hereafter timeously (at the proper time) delivered.''

Since there was no further reference to either ''dimension'' or ''plan'', the problem was not resolved until the answer was revealed in a bill for paving the Square in 1814. From measurements of each quadrant of masonry, it was possible to plot the paved area of the Square. The resulting diagram showed three voids...one marking the site of the court house, one for the Market erected in 1767, and one for the Public Office Building constructed in 1792-94. Thus, the unpaved sections represented the dimensions of those buildings. Allowing 18 inches on each side of the Court House, on the North-South axis, for the customary brick drainage area, the dimensions proved to be 45' x 45', instead of the 55' x 45' previously accepted.

Digging for Facts

This discrepancy gave rise to one of the most dramatic, if unscheduled events of the Bicentennial Calendar. Friday, May 23, 1975 is remembered as THE DAY THEY DUG UP THE SQUARE. Which was right? The 55' x 45' of the York County History or the newly calculated 45' x 45'? There was only one way to find out. Look and see! Accordingly, in the presence of City officials, reporters, and Bicentennial representatives including the building architect and contractors, a small trench was excavated 22-1/2 feet west of the precise center of the Square. And there it was...the stone foundation wall of the Provincial Court House, just where William Willis had built it 221 years before. The true and indisputable dimensions were 45 x 45 feet.

Although there was no further occasion to ''dig for the truth'' in such a literal fashion, the search for right answers continued. There must be no guess work, and the questions were coming thick and fast. ''How deep?''...''How wide?''...''How high?''...''What color?'' Sometimes the answer to one question posed a host of others. For example: "Was there a bell?" The answer was "Yes." In April of 1769 the Commissioners agreed to have a bell bought for the use of the public to be hung in the Court House. On May 28, 1769 the Commissioners received the bell, which cost 55 pounds, 15 shillings, four pence and ordered it hung in the cupola. But where was it purchased? Where was it manufactured and what became of it when the court house was torn down? Had it been salvaged from the wreckage? Had it been transferred to the new court house, or, to some other public building? The search was on!

The trail led over rooftops, up stairways and steeples. The bell in the present court house? Too large! The one in the Laurel Fire Company Engine House? Wrong date. Although the missing bell was never found, the search was not in vain. Responding to a newspaper inquiry — "Who's Got the Bell?" — a member of the community long interested in the preservation of York history, donated a suitable and significant substitute — the handsome bronze bell, dated 1805, from York County's first almshouse.

Almshouse and Hospital at Little York drawn by Wm. Wagner, 1800-1869

Courtesy of Hist. Soc. of York Co.

This particular bell, a collector's item in its own right, has survived as the sole reminder of York's involvement in a tragic incident of American history. At the beginning of the War of 1812, Light-Horse Harry Lee, father of Robert E. Lee, was the victim of a political riot in Baltimore. Beaten and mutilated almost beyond recognition, this American patriot who coined the description of Washington as "First in war, first in peace, and first in the hearts of his countrymen", was given up for dead. But some solicitous friends smuggled him out of the city to "Little York" where he was treated by Dr. John Spangler at the Almhouse Hospital. Today the same bell which rang in a new life for an American Revolutionary General, rings in a new beginning for an American Revolutionary building.

Dr. John Spangler
1770-1851

As work on the interior of the new court house progressed, the questions multiplied. How was the building lighted and heated? What color were the walls? What were the furnishings? How were they arranged? The answers came from a variety of sources. The county treasury accounts showed bills for candles and firewood, for whitewashing the interior, for black paint for baseboards. In a letter written by Henry Laurens, who had somewhat reluctantly succeeded John Hancock as President of Continental Congress, he made the comment: "I may as well sit president as any other Character — A good seat near a warm fire must compensate for additional labor . . . ."

The stove, therefore, must have been positioned near the Bench of Justice. And, by great good fortune, the bench itself was still in existence, having been acquired by The Historical Society of York County in 1948. This treasured relic of the original court house was designed to accommodate three or four Justices presiding over the same court at the same time, as was the colonial custom. It bears the added distinction of being the oldest bench in the country to have been occupied by Presidents of Congress, as those in Philadelphia, Baltimore and Lancaster were destroyed by fire.

The figure of Justice, carved by John Fisher in 1796, had also survived the vandalism of 1841, and, as the property of the York County Bar Association, was restored to its rightful place above the official dais.

In general, the furniture was selected and arranged to recreate the proper setting for the deliberations of Continental Congress in 1777-78. To seat 13 congressional delegations in so small a court room, the jury benches had been pushed back against the walls and extra tables and chairs were borrowed from the townspeople to accommodate the more than thirty

Setting the Stage

11

delegates sometimes in attendance. So crowded was the space between the Justices' Bench and the railing, that four delegations were seated in the outer area normally open to the public. The hand-crafted reproductions of tables and chairs in assorted styles of the period, the candle holders and writing utensils, even such accessories as foot-warmers, floor-length table covers, ballot box, leather fire buckets, wood box for the four plate cast-iron stove, and a lantern to light the path to the outdoor "necessaries" were approved only after careful study.

The Journals of Congress and letters from delegates supplied many specific and interesting details: the placement and equipment of the Secretary's table: the location of the doorkeeper's chair, occupied during the York sojourn by Martin Breneise, who was also responsible for tending the fire, supplying the candles, and ringing the court house bell; the traditional seating of delegates from North to South, according to the states they represented; the existence and importance of a map table.

"Where Justice steadied her scales."
Bench, clock and Figure of Justice from original court room.

Photo by Don Lehman

The one piece of furniture which probably contributed most dramatically to the interpretation of the room, and the great events associated with it, was the original tall-case clock which had ticked off the minutes and sounded the hours of those momentous congressional sessions. Godfrey Lenhart, who made this historic timepiece, was one of York's earliest and finest clockmakers, well known for his beautiful cabinet work. But "#30" was housed in a plain, almost primitive, walnut case, indicating, no doubt, the economy minded commissioners who had ordered it for the court house. When it was auctioned off at the public sale of 1841, Dr. Jacob Hay, a lineal descendant of Colonel John Hay of the Revolution, was the highest bidder. The old clock was handed down as a family heirloom from one generation to another, until in 1975 it was purchased from Jacob L. Hay, the fifth, well known journalist and short story writer, and returned to what might be considered its "ancestral home."

Even before the building was completed, it began to capture the interest and imagination of the people. They watched the heightening of the walls, the placement of doors and windows, the hanging of the shutters, the roofing operation . . . with more than casual interest. The past was coming closer. But the court house would not be the court house without the cupola and "Little General" weathervane.

The original weathervane, as befitted a court house of the King, was the broad gilded arrow symbolizing British sovereignty. But, the story goes that a group of patriots, fired by the public reading of the Declaration of Independence in the Court House Square, tore down this offending arrow as a demonstration of their new-found freedom from the Crown. The weathercock, which is said to have supplanted the English arrow, was, in its turn, battered to bits by stray militiamen who used it for target practice, and was eventually replaced by John Fisher's likeness of a Polish Dragoon, inspired by the presence of Count Pulaski and his Legion in 1779. This quaint, helmeted figure with drawn sabre was affectionately known as "The Little Man" or "Little General" and came to be York's best known and best loved relic of the Revolution.

Which way the wind blows!

By April 17, 1976, the sparkling white cupola, surmounted by a hand-crafted copy of the Little General, so perfect as to be indistinguishable from the original, was ready to be hoisted into place. Watching the scene was like watching a slow-motion re-run of the 1841 demolition, shown backwards. At the York Centennial of 1887, seventy eight year old William Beitzel had recorded his personal recollections:

"I remember the old court house very well, and was one of those who helped pull down its steeple when the structure was demolished. The steeple fell on the lower side of George Street, the "little man" on top of it falling back and into the doorway of the court house where it was picked up uninjured, and is now, I believe, in the possession of the Laurel Engine Company."

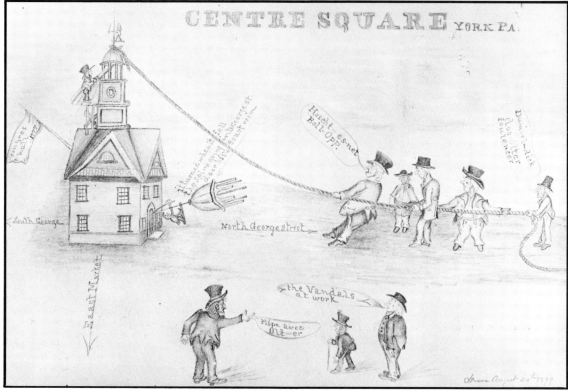

Drawing by David Heckert, 1825-1908

Courtesy of Hist. Soc. of York Co.

Now the scene was re-enacted in reverse — not "what goes up must come down"...but rather..."what came down must go up!" To the spectators and public at large this return of the Little General to his post provided the court house with a fifth dimension of reality. Gradually — almost imperceptibly — the new building assumed the identity of the old. Separated by two city blocks and two centuries, the two structures were merging into one.

To present-day visitors there is no longer a difference in time and place. The union is complete. "Here" the gentlemen of Congress assembled; "Here" the Articles of Confederation were adopted. "Here" the day of National Thanksgiving was first proclaimed. "Here" occurred the other great events which shaped the nation.

In a new age, in new accents, and with a new voice the building speaks. And the people listen.

Raising the cupola, April 17, 1976

Dedication May 1, 1976
Heavy rain made it no place for the "Summer Soldier or Sunshine Patriot"

Voices of Bench, Bar and Ballots

It seems to be singularly appropriate that May First, nationally cele-brated as Law Day, should have been the date chosen for the dedication of ''York County's Heritage Gift to the Nation''.

A nation's heritage is both tangible and intangible. It is the land . . . the forests and mountains, the plains and valleys; it is the long reaches of lakes and rivers and the rich black deposits beneath the crust of the earth; it is the log cabins, the New England ''Salt Boxes'', the pillared mansions of the Old South . . . the little red schoolhouses and ''Cathedrals of Learning'' . . . the spires and steeples of churches . . . the lofty domes of Public Buildings; it is the people and other customs, their arts and industries, their achievements and sacrifices.

But a nation's heritage is also its convictions . . . its faith . . . its ideals . . . its dreams and promises. It has been said that America's roots are less in soil than in parchment. From that first document of human freedom, the Magna Charta (1215), guaranteeing the liberties of the individual, eventu-ally came two great American documents — the Declaration of a nation's right to determine its own destiny and a constitution designed ''to secure the blessings of liberty to ourselves and our posterity.''

Thus America's heritage of freedom is based upon the heritage of common law. And it was the individual's right to the protection of law and access to the courts which prompted the inhabitants of the western part of Lancaster County to petition the Provincial Assembly for the erection of a new county west of the Susquehanna.

The Petitioners pointed out the "great hardship of being so great a distance from the Borough of Lancaster where the Courts of Justice were held and the Public Offices were kept." They further indicated the difficulty of securing themselves against thefts and other abuses perpetrated by "idle and dissolute persons" who, too easily, escaped justice by reason of that great distance from a court or prison. It was to remedy these inconveniences and provide a means of maintaining law and order that the petition was granted in 1749.

So essential to individual freedom was this right of access to the law, that Thomas Jefferson included its violation among the 27 charges against the King, submitted in the "Declaration of Independence to a candid world."

> *"He (King George III) has called together Legislative Bodies at Places unusual, uncomfortable, and distant from the Repository of their Public Records, for the sole purpose of fatiguing them into Compliance with his Measures."*

And even more specifically he blamed the reigning monarch

> *"For transporting us beyond the Seas to be tried for pretended Offences."*

But the erection of York County provided the inhabitants with their own judicial system by establishing the Court of Quarter Sessions and General Gaol Delivery and the County Court of Common Pleas. The same Provincial Assembly Act which defined the boundaries of the new county also provided for the appointment of duly competent Justices, and authorized the election of two representatives to the Assembly, these elections to be held "at or near the Place where the Court House is intended to be built for the said County."

Although Articles VI of this same document authorized Thomas Cox, Michael Tanner, George Swope, Nathan Hussey and John Wright, Junior (or any three of them) to purchase a "piece of Land situate in some Convenient Place in the said County . . . . . and thereon to erect and build a Court-House and Prison", it would appear from the previous statement that the "Convenient Place" had already been determined.

Actually, it is a matter of record that the idea of a second county beyond the Susquehanna, the selection of York as the County Seat, and the site of the court house had all been decided long before the events of 1749.

Reporting at the February term of the Lancaster Court in 1742, the surveyors appointed to lay out "a round by the nearest way, from the town in Great Codorus to William Smith's Patented Land under Maryland", had described its northern terminus as "the end of the street (George) leading to the place intended for a court house in the town of York."

These surveyors must have been familiar with the original plan of York, laid out some six months earlier by Thomas Cookson, Deputy Surveyor of Lancaster County. Cookson had faithfully followed what was known as the "Philadelphia Plan" by plotting the new town in a geometric pattern, "two streets 80 feet wide (George and Market) to cross each other, and 65 feet square to be cut off the corner of each lot to make sure a square for any public building or market of 110 feet each side."

"The Philadelphia Plan"

In 1743, James Logan, Secretary of the Province, writing to Thomas Penn on the progress of York Town, then consisting of eleven houses, anticipated the separation of the two counties in the statement: "The prospect of its being a county seat some time or other pleases most of the people."

A French traveler, Theophile Cazanove, visiting York in 1794, made the comment: "The court house, placed in the middle of the square, ridiculously shuts off the view of the whole of the two main streets." But ridiculous as it may have seemed to the Frenchman, the Penn concept of the center of law as the center of a community was responsible for the location of the Court House at the head of Market Street in Philadelphia, in the center of town at Lancaster, in the very center of Fifth and Penn Streets in Reading, and, as late as 1800, in the center of the Square at Gettysburg.

The Penns were planners, business men, who knew from experience that public roads affected the growth of towns along their route. By creating the Court House Square at the intersection of the East-West, North-South highways they were establishing a hub of trade and commerce in a wilderness area; and in 1749 York County was little more than that.

The Commissioners, charged by the Assembly with the responsibility of raising the necessary funds to purchase the land and build the court house and prison, were so confounded by the lack of resources that they took their problem to the Proprietaries of the Province. In a petition addressed to Thomas and Richard Penn they pled their case:

> *"Foreasmuch as this County (but a few years since) was an uncultivated Wilderness, and even now the greatest Number of Settlements are but little improved, and what Produce we make its chiefly consum'd by the*

Expence of its Carriage to navigable Water, and as the Publick Buildings immediately necessary will occasion a heavy Tax, which under these Circumstances will be difficult to bear, We therefore (in behalf of the County aforesaid) humbly pray your Honours to take our Case under Consideration, and contribute what your Honours please towards defraying the charge of the aforesaid Buildings."

It must have been a keen disappointment to the Petitioners, that their "Honours" were not "pleased to contribute" anything at all towards the proposed buildings. Nor was there any assistance forthcoming from the Provincial Assembly. Although later records show that loans were advanced for court houses and prisons to Bedford, Westmoreland and Northampton, York County was left to shift for itself. Accordingly, on November 26, 1753 the Board of Commissioners agreed to raise the sum of 504 pounds, 16 shillings and five pence on the following tax plan:

"For every hundred acres of good land, the sum of ten pounds, middling to the sum of eight pounds; for every acre of winter grane, the sum of ten shillings; for every bonded servant the sum of eight pounds; for every negro, the sum of ten pounds; horned cattle, the sum of thirty shillings; for horses and mares, the sum of four pounds; sheep, the sum of two shillings and six pence."

"The gladsome light of Jurisprudence." Sir Edward Coke

Meanwhile, the town was growing. The count of 47 dwellings in 1749 had risen to 210 by 1754, as more and more families sought the economic opportunities and protection of the County Seat. In the interim between the erection of the County and the completion of the court house, the courts were held in private houses, most likely in the homes of George Swope and George Stevenson, who, together with John Day, Thomas Cox, John Wright, Junior, Matthew Dill, Hance Hamilton and Patrick Watson were commissioned through royal authority by the Governor of the Province as the first Justices of York County.

The first Court of Quarter Sessions convened on October 31, 1749 with John Day presiding and the following day the first Orphan's Court was held before Justices Day, Cox and Watson.

Although these early Courts are not, strictly speaking, a part of the Court House history, their structure, personnel, cases and business are pertinent to the over-all story in so far as they portray the life and times of the era. It may be noted, for example, that of the first eight appointed Justices, only one, George Stevenson, was a member of the Bar. Until the

State Convention of 1790 it was not necessary for a Court Justice to be a lawyer or to possess any particular or technical knowledge of the law. Justices were chosen for their good judgment, business experience, personal integrity and community influence. Their decisions were based on the arguments presented by the prosecuting and defense attorneys from whom they acquired sufficient knowledge of legal principles and their application to dispense justice with what has been described as "a comparatively even hand."

The scarcity of well educated men in these sparsely populated settlements required a man of even modest scholastic attainments "to wear more than one hat!". Thus we find two Justices of 1749, George Swope and Patrick Watson, doubling as County Commissioners. A third Justice, Hance Hamilton, also served as Sheriff, and George Stevenson played the triple role of Justice, Prothonatary and Clerk of the Courts. As a qualified lawyer and Surveyor, Stevenson's services were in such great demand throughout the Province that he was, more often than not, excused from his judicial duties, although he frequently appeared as Prosecutor for the Crown.

On January 7, 1750, this busy and talented man assumed new duties *Riding the Range* and a new title, when James Hamilton, Deputy Governor of Pennsylvania, appointed him "Chief Ranger of and for the County of York." The job description, originally quoted by Carter and Glossbrenner in their HISTORY OF YORK COUNTY, provides further insight into the reaches and jurisdiction of provincial law.

Stevenson's commission as Chief Ranger granted him

> *"full power and authority to range, view and inspect all our woods and lands within the said county, and to seize, take up and appropriate to our use all and every such wild colts or young horses, cattle, and swine, as shall be found within the bounds of said county, that are not marked by the owners of their dams, and are liable to be seized by law; and also all marked strays for which no lawful owner can be found, that may be taken up in the said county; and to publish every such stray in the most public places of the said county for the space of one year, and also keeping some public mark of their being strays for the said space about them, hereby requiring you to sue and prosecute all persons presuming to act contrary to law in cutting down or destroying any of our timber trees or wood, or that shall any wise invade the powers hereby granted you within the said county."*

From this document alone, it is easy to understand the necessity for "free and easy access to the courts." The farmers of York County would, indeed, have been hard pressed to journey across the Susquehanna to register their live stock in the court house at Lancaster. As it was, the early records of York Quarter Sessions contain such entries as:

"Moses Wallace of Chanceford Township, his marks for cattle, horses, sheep and swine &c a crop on the left ear &c. Brand an I on the near shoulder and buttocks. April 25, 1751."

"James Hetrick, his marks, a crop and slit on the off ear. Brand a fleur-de-luce on the rear buttocks. May 2, 1751."

The business before those first York County Courts was, in part, dictated by the existing laws of the Province, but was also structured to meet the needs of a pioneer people. The proper organization of the County demanded the appointment of Commissioners, Assessors, and Township Constables. In the absence of such facilities as a workhouse, almshouse, even a jail, it was necessary for the Court to appoint Overseers of the Poor to serve in the 25 existing townships. Increasing trade called for closer supervision of highways and added accommodations for travelers, necessitating the court recommendation of suitable persons as innkeepers and proprietors of "Public Houses of Entertainment." In the interest of law and order, the courts of 1750 required all tavern keepers to give their bond "to suffer no drunkenness, unlawful gaming or any other disturbance", and, even more important, "to sell no intoxicating drink to Indians to debauch or hurt them."

To protect the public against excessive rates imposed by greedy tavern owners, each county was required by the Assembly to establish its own price controls by court action. Accordingly, the following rates were settled by the court and proclaimed by the Crier in open Court of Quarter Session, January 28, 1752.

	s.	d.	
One quart of sangaree made with one pint of good maderia wine and with loaf sugar	1	6	
A bowl of punch made with one quart of water with loaf sugar and good Jamacia spirits	1	6	
One pint good Maderia wine	1	3	
One pint good Vidonia wine	O	10	
One pint good Port wine	1	O	
One quart of mimbo made with West India rum and loaf sugar	O	10	
One quart of mimbo made with New England rum and loaf sugar	O	9	
One gill of good West India rum	O	4	
One gill of good New England rum	O	3	
One gill of good whiskey................................	O	2	
One quart of good beer	O	4	
One quart of good cider.................................	O	4	
One man's breakfast	O	6	
One man's dinner	O	8	
One man's supper	O	6	
One horse at hay twenty-four hours	O	10	
One horse at hay one night..............................	O	8	
Half a gallon of good oats	O	3	

"s." indicates Shillings (14c) "d." indicates Denari (pennies)

Despite their general disposition toward law and order, the early inhabitants of York County were not always of such peaceable persuasion. Tempers were quick to flare among the German, English, Scotch, Irish and Welsh settlers, and when they did, there could be spilled blood and broken heads. In 1749 the antagonism between the "Dutch" and Irish exploded into a fury which turned the county's first election into a Battle for the Ballot Box. The log house of Baltzer Spangler on Lot #70 in the Square was chosen as the most central location for the polls. The actual ballot depository was a space between the logs of the unfinished dwelling. All went well until the Irish supporters of Hance Hamilton for Sheriff attempted to stop the

Buffets and Ballots

German supporters of the rival candidate, Richard McAlister, from casting their votes. Two or three stalwart Irishmen guarding this primitive polling place were suddenly tripped up and sent sprawling by an infuriated German determined to cast his ballot. The fight was on. Fists flew. Both sides armed themselves with saplings growing nearby, and with these cudgels belabored each other without mercy until the Irish forces were completely routed and driven well beyond the Codorus. This left the German party in possession of the polls, and McAlister was, if not duly, at least forcibly, elected. Unfortunately for the "Democratic Process", the Deputy Governor saw fit to overturn the election results and commission the loser, Hance Hamilton, as first Sheriff of York County.

Resentment was still in the air the following year at the election of Representatives to the Assembly, and again the antagonism between the two factions erupted into a full scale riot. Hance Hamilton, in his capacity as Sheriff, attempted to restore order, was knocked down. As angry mob, armed with sticks, stones, and brickbats, stormed the voting place, broke the windows and forced Hamilton and the election inspectors to escape by way of a rear window. The Germans then captured the ballot box and refused to surrender it, thereby preventing any official returns.

This time the affair was brought before the Assembly in November of 1750. Charges and counter-charges were made, each side blaming the other for the unseemly fracas. The Germans, although not entirely vindicated, at least had the satisfaction of hearing Hamilton receive an official reprimand from the Speaker in which he was admonished to preserve better order in the future. On the local scene, the whole election was written off by the following decisions of the October Court of Quarter Sessions:

> *"It is therefore considered and ordered by the Court here (York) that the commissioners and assessors who served this county in their several stations last year, shall serve for the ensuing year, or until there shall be a new election."*

"Order in the court!"

But violence was the exception rather than the rule. The Courts were conducted with all due decorum by Justices who upheld the dignity of their office and saw to it that witnesses, jurors and spectators conducted themselves as befitted the sovereignty of the law. When in 1750 a frustrated witness so far forgot himself as to deliver a barrage of profanity, he was promptly fined. And, again in 1752 when an irate Grand Juror, named Charles Crimm, enlivened the scene by hurling a glass of wine in the face of a fellow juror, the court immediately collected twenty shillings.

By the time the court house was under construction (1754) the county was well established, the courts were functioning, and even the most remote and isolated homesteader had some sense of being under the protection of the law. A man could get title to his land, probate a will, protect his property, obtain a license to buy and sell, clear himself of indenture, collect his just debts, swear out a complaint against an offending neighbor, or haul a criminal to justice without the undue hardship and expense of a long and hazardous journey. Even women and bondsmen had certain legal rights.

"Laws are the very Bulwarks of liberty."
J. C. Holland

Gottlieb Mittelberger, warning his countrymen of the inequities of English law suffered by German settlers, and the evils of the indenture system by which men were forced to sell themselves and their families into servitude for passage money, was thoroughly shocked by the liberties accorded to females in Pennsylvania. "I'd rather get into a fight with three men in England", he wrote, "then give an Englishwoman a slap in the face! When her own husband boxes her ears, and she complains to the neighboring women, his life is no longer safe. If it happens several times, he had better put a safe distance between himself and her, or she can see to it that he is put into prison for a long time." He was further outraged that a woman could bring suit, and testify in court. "In court the evidence of one Englishwoman is worth that of three male witnesses. It is said that Englishwomen received this great privilege from Queen Elizabeth."

The indenture system, admittedly one of the blackest chapters in the annals of Pennsylvania, did not mean total slavery. Redemptioners "worked out their time" under a legal agreement and had recourse to the courts for redress against their masters for abuse, ill-treatment, injustice, or any other breach of contract.

Clearly the construction of a county court house was of real significance to all the inhabitants — men and women — bound or free. But whatever rejoicing the new building may have occasioned was overshadowed by the stark terror and tragedy of the French and Indian War.

Accustomed to William Penn's policy of peaceful co-existence with the Indians, the people of York County were ill informed of the mounting tensions caused by the French and English power plays on the western frontier, and ill prepared for attack.

The court house was barely under roof when, in April of 1755, Benjamin Franklin arrived in York Town to contract for baggage wagons and horses, desperately needed by General Braddock, who had recently arrived from England with two regiments, under orders to assist the Provincial troops in driving the French from Fort Duquesne. With characteristic shrewdness, Franklin appealed to pocketbooks rather than patriotism, offering 15 shillings a day for each wagon with four horses and driver, 2 shillings a day for each able horse with a packsaddle, and 18 pence a day for any unsaddled horse. The further promise of seven days' advance pay, full restitution for wagons and animals lost en route, and the assurance that drivers would be exempt from soldiering, sweetened the pot. Besides, as Franklin took pains to point out, it was only common sense to contribute for profit what would surely be confiscated by force, should the quota not be filled.

This two-edged persuasion brought results. Within two weeks 150 wagons and 259 pack horses were crossing the Alleghennies with the ill-fated expedition. In July Braddock's defeat and the total disaster near Fort Duquesne left the frontier unprotected and opened the way for a full scale invasion by marauding Indians. As the bloody trail of the tomahawk cut through the Cumberland Valley, where settlers abandoned their farms and fled for their lives, the terror mounted in York County.

News of a sizeable encampment along the Susquehanna within a short march of John Harris's Ferry threatened to wipe out a virtually helpless population. It was the York magistrates who shouldered the responsibility for the town defenses. George Stevenson, John Adlum, Herman Updegraff, James Smith and Thomas Armor, all Court Justices, dispatched an urgent plea to Governor Robert Hunter Morris. Stevenson's letter, written at eleven o'clock on the night of November First, reveals the urgency of the situation:

> "We believe there are men enough willing to bear Arms & go out against the Enemy, were they supplied with Arms, Ammunition & a reasonable Allowance for their time, but without this, at least arms and Ammunition, we feel little to purpose can be done.
>
> If some measures are not speedily fallen upon, we must either sit at home till we are butcher'd without Mercy or resistance, run away, or go away, a confused Multitude destitute of Arms and Ammunition & without discipline or proper Officers, or any way fixed on to be supplied with Provisions.
>
> In short we know not what to do, & have not much time to deliberate.
>
> As the Company who go, from this Town and Parts adjacent, to Morrow, to the assistance of the Inhabitants of our Frontiers, will take almost all our Arms & Ammunition with them, We humbly pray your Honour to order us some Arms & Ammunition, otherwise we must desert our Habitations."

That no relief was forthcoming from an apathetic Assembly is evidenced by a letter to Judge Richard Peters (Philadelphia) in which Stevenson even more vividly describes York's desperate plight:

> "We have sent 53 Men well filed, from this Town last Monday 2 o'clock P.M. & a Doctor, some Medicines & what Ammunitions we could spare to Tobs Hendrick's to join the main Body of English Tories on the most needful Part of the Frontiers. Mr. Adlum (Justice) is with them. Mr. Hamilton (Sheriff) is gone towards Conigogeeg (near Chambersburg) last Sunday with a Company.
>
> Mr. Bay (Justice) with & at the Head of another. We are all aloft and such as have Arms hold themselves ready, but, alas, they are few in Number; 40 men came here yesterday willing to defend, but had but 3 guns and no Ammunition, and could get none here, therefore went home again.
>
> We stay all here yet, how long God knows. Six Families fled from their Homes, Dist. about 15 miles viz: Conewago Last Night, the last came into Town about Day Break This Morning. I am determined to stay & by the assistance of Mr. Lispy & the other Justices, on the spot spirit up the People & keep 'em together (if possible) till I hear from the Government."

It was in this period of panic and general upheaval that the Court House in the Square was finally completed (1756) and opened its doors to a people plagued by war and besieged by fear. Action taken at the Court of Quarter Sessions for April, 1758 reflects the temper of the times:

> *"Upon the Petition of sundrie of the Inhabitants of the Frontier Townships of this County setting forth the Murders, Ravages and Captivity that have lately been committed on some of the late Inhabitants of the said Townships and that many of their Neighbors have removed from their respective Habitations to the Interior Parts of the County; That the Petitioners & their Neighbors have kept Guards on the Frontiers ever since the said Murders have been committed, and praying some Assistance from the Interior Parts of the County &c, was read after mature consideration tis agreed as follows:*
>> *"That forty five men be immediately rais'd, maintained and paid at the Expense of this County, to be divided into three Companies consisting of fifteen Men, each one of which to have the command of the other fourteen which said Men are to patrol along the Frontiers of this County for the Defence and Protection of the Inhabitants thereof.*

Although the immediate danger of large scale Indian attacks had passed, sporadic raids and acts of terrorism continued within York County until the end of the war from which England emerged as the most powerful nation on earth.

"The King is dead!"

"Long Live the King!"

The year 1760 was marked by an event which created little excitement at the time, but which was to have a profound affect on the lives and fortunes of all American colonists. King George II, deservedly remembered as "The Best of the Georges", died at the age of seventy seven, and was succeeded by his twenty two year old grandson, the first English born and English educated monarch of the Hanoverian line. To the farmers of York County, especially the Pennsylvania Germans, who comprised three fourths of the population, one king was very like another. It mattered little who wore the crown so long as he was 3,000 miles away and stayed there. And in the Court House the only change in procedure occasioned by the new reign was the substitution of "George III" for "George II" in the formal phraseology of legal documents, records and the oath of allegiance. Otherwise, it was business as usual. The court calendars were crowded and so was the new prison (completed in the same year as the court house) on the north east corner of George and King Street.

The jail population consisted largely of felons, debtors and runaway bondsmen awaiting trial. Thanks to William Penn's liberal views on religious freedom, no man could be persecuted or prosecuted for his faith, and Penn's own religious convictions were responsible for some modification of the Penal Code. In Pennsylvania the death penalty was imposed only for murder, treason, and counterfeiting, whereas in England, and in some of the colonies, there were more than 200 offences for which a man could be executed.

King George II 1683-1760, during whose reign York was founded in 1741 and for whom George Street was named.

But Pennsylvania criminal laws were, by no means, lenient, and the punishments meted out at the Provincial Court House were certainly not "blessed" by any "quality of Mercy." Old records show that Margaret Wilmouth received fifteen lashes for stealing a silk handkerchief. A man who was guilty of stealing a linen shirt and a pair of stockings suffered the same punishment plus twelve days in jail for the cost of prosecution. A convicted rapist was sentenced to 21 lashes, a fine of five pounds and one hour in the pillory.

By far the most severe penalty was reserved for persons who dared tamper with The King's Coin. Although actual counterfeiting was punishable by "death without benefit of clergy", the man or woman who changed the denomination of a note was subject to the most inhuman cruelty the law could devise. In 1768 James Pitt was tried by Andrew Allen, Attorney General, for altering a two shilling bill of credit to a ten shilling note. He was convicted and sentenced to have both his ears cut off and nailed to the pillory in which he was to stand for one hour, also to receive 39 lashes, well laid on, and pay a fine of 100 pounds, one half to go to the Governor of the Province, the other to his informant. Since the poor wretch was penniless, he was further sentenced to be sold into servitude for a period of four years, his purchase price to be similarly divided.

Selling individuals to defray court costs, as part of a criminal sentence, or as payment to creditors was a common practice. A man imprisoned for indebtedness had the right to sell himself, or his children, to obtain his release. The punishment of runaway bondservants was an extension of their term of indenture, determined by the duration of their escape, the expenses incurred by their masters during their absence, and the cost of getting them back. The York County Continuance Docket for July of 1769 contains the following entry:

> *"Upon the application of Baltzer Spangler, Junior, to this court setting forth that his Servant Man named Robert Gamel Hath, without his leave, absented himself from his Service two different times for the Space of twenty one days, and that he hath been obliged to expend, in taking him up, and having him brought home, thirteen Pounds, 17 shillings and 6 Pence, and Praying the Court to order the Said Servant to make him Satisfaction for the said Runaway Time and expences, and the said Robert Gamel, also being present in Court, and hearing what he had to say in his own defence, It is Considered by the Court and adjudged That the said Robert Gamel serve the said Baltzer Spangler or his Assigns after the*

Expiration of the Time mentioned in his Indenture, for and during the term of Two Years in full satisfaction of his Runaway Time and Expences.''

In the July Term of 1770 a certain Thomas Haughy accused by his master of having run away for two months and eleven days, and also of stealing and destroying his original Indenture, voluntarily entered into a new agreement for a period of seven years . . . surely a high price to pay for so brief a liberty!

Even more revealing than the actual court records are the detailed bills and expense accounts submitted to the County of Gaolers and Sheriffs directly responsible for the custody of prisoners. All services are carefully itemized:

Counting the Cost

> *"Victualing'' (feeding) a prisoner . . . from 5 shillings a week to 6 or 9 pence a day*
> *For Turning the Key . . . 5 shillings*
> *For Putting one man in irons . . . 2 shillings, 6 pence*
> *For Removing irons . . . 2 shillings, 6 pence*
> *Repairing chains and making handcuffs . . . 1 pound, 5 shillings*

A bill submitted by Sheriff David McConaughy in 1769 shows that each whipping cost the County 10 shillings. During the period covered by his statement, four of the flogging victims were women, and one man, Richard Healy made two trips to the dreaded post as a repeat offender. The accounts of Sheriff William Bailey (1786) show a sliding scale of five to ten shillings, depending, no doubt, on the number of lashes. Ear cropping was extra!

Similar accounts tell of expenses incurred by York County's version of a "Chain Gang"

> *"For Supervising Men sentenced to the Wheelbarrows from September 13th to October 13th, 1788 . . . 5 pounds, 5 shillings*
> *Another entry: "For mending Wheelbarrow Men's chains . . . 4 shillings:*
> *and yet another: "For Making Four Shirts for Barrow Men . . . 6 shillings."*

The whole pitiful story of Elisabeth Irwin, executed for murder in 1765, is related in Pounds, Shillings and Pence. Her "Diet" for 19 weeks and six days, according to her Gaoler, Jacob Greybill, came to 4 Pounds, 17 Shillings. Sheriff Robert McPherson, in charge of the execution, itemizes the whole procedure:

> *"To Cash paid for making a Gallows for the Execution*
>
> *of Elisabeth Irwin . . . . 1 Pound*

To Cash for a Rope . . . . *7 Shills. 6 Pence*

To a Cart and Horse . . . . *1 Pound*

To Cash paid the Hangman . . . . *5 Pounds*

To My Expences in bring the Hangman
 and returning him to Lancaster . . . . *5 Pounds, 7 Shills.*
 8 Pence

To Cash Paid for a Coffin . . . . *15 Shillings*

To Digging the Grave . . . . *15 Shillings*

Elisabeth Irwin's Tryal Fees . . . . *8 Pounds, 8 Shills.*
 6 Pence

The total cost of her execution, some 25 pounds, probably exceeded any single sum of money expended on Elisabeth Irwin during her entire lifetime.

But if the "wages of sin" were death, mortal suffering and public humiliation, the rewards of Jury Duty were much more pleasurable, as indicated by the following statement:

TRAVERSE JURY AND CONSTABLES BILL TO G. HAY

		Pounds	*Shills.*	*Pence*
	to 3-1/2 bottles Madiera Wine	1	3	5
	to 2 pints Brandy & Spirits		7	6
	to 15 suppers	1	10	
Sept. 5th	1-1/2 Bottles Holland Gin		8	5
	to 15 Breakfasts	1	10	
	to Lodging		15	
	to 2 Bottles Madiera		15	
	to 15 Dinners	1	17	6
	to one Quart Spirits		7	6
	to 4 Bottles Madiera	1	10	
6th	to 1/2 Pint Holland Gin		1	10-1/2
		10	6	2-1/2

Court Days in York Town, as in most rural communities, were special occasions for people whose dawn to dusk routine of heavy farm labor offered little change of pace or variety. Families came to town to visit, transact business and exchange news and views with folks from other parts of the County. The public benches in the court room were usually filled with spectators who also attended executions, witnessed floggings and hurled their share of insults and rotten eggs at the helpless occupants of the pillory in the Court House Square.

That some of these same upright citizens were not above turning a dishonest shilling at the expense of the county is illustrated by documents pertaining to the payment of bounty for wolf heads. When it became apparent that some farmers were collecting several times over for the same grisly evidence of their kill, the Commissioners passed a special ruling that every head presented for bounty must straightway be burned in front of the court house door!

But despite the crudeness of the time, the harshness of frontier life, primitive living conditions and the free flow of hard liquor in taverns and at such "social events" as weddings and funerals, the moral tone of York County in the 18th century was highly acceptable. Labor was honorable, idleness a sin, and lawlessness was severely discouraged both by the courts and by the church. The pioneer families of English, Scotch-Irish and German origin who settled here were deeply and sincerely religious. Their personal conduct was governed by their conscience and the discipline of their faith.

The growth and prosperity of a town could be measured by the number *Decade of Progress* of churches and improvements to church property. Within ten years after the building of the court house, both the German Lutheran and Reformed churches, originally of logs, were replaced by stone, the Moravian and Episcopal congregations had constructed their places of worship and the Society of Friends had erected the Meeting House which is still in use on West Philadelphia Street.

The late 1700's were busy years for the county commissioners responsible for meeting the needs of an expanding community. The wooden span across the Codorus on West Market Street was replaced by a substantial stone bridge. The walls of the old jail having been declared unsafe, a more adequate building was erected to serve as both prison and workhouse. The Square itself took on a new look with the construction of a market shed to the west of the court house. This was a project long overdue, as York had been granted the privilege of holding market twice a week (Wednesdays and Saturdays) by Thomas and Richard Penn in 1755. The completion of this facility in 1768 was a stimulus to growth and prosperity. York, as a thriving market town and County Seat, began to attract residents from other areas who saw in its bustling taverns, busy shops and well attended churches new opportunities for personal advancement and leadership.

Voices of Protest

A Call To Arms

By the latter half of the 18th Century, the Court House was dominated by new faces and new voices. When George Stevenson resigned his post as Prothonotary in 1764, after 16 years of service, the Provincial Authority appointed as his successor York's first resident lawyer, Samuel Johnston. Johnston, admitted to the Bar in 1755, had been born and educated in England. He was an able lawyer, a representative of the Penn Heirs and a loyal subject of the King. His knowledge of the law, his widespread practice, and his skill as an orator won him a reputation which attracted aspiring students to seek his tutelage.

One of these students-at-law was James Smith, second son of an Irish immigrant, whose previous study with his brother George in Lancaster, together with his natural wit and jovial personality, stood him in good stead as a practicing attorney. When Johnston's duties as Prothonotary, Clerk of the Courts, Register of Wills and Recorder of Deeds forced him to retire from active practice, James Smith was the only other member of the Bar.

But another Johnston protegee was admitted in 1769. This was Thomas Hartley, who, as a lad of 18 had come from Berks County to read law with the distinguished relative of his mother. Hartley was one of the few bilingual lawyers in the Province. His fluency in their native tongue, endeared him to the Pennsylvania Germans to whom the language barrier had long been a source of dissatisfaction with English justice as administered by English courts.

Samuel Johnston, 1727-1810,
Tory Tutor of Patriots

A less dedicated but no less articulate student, young Alexander Graydon, rescued from the pitfalls of Philadelphia by an anxious uncle in the summer of 1773, later described the circumstances of his arrival in York and his association with the learned Mr. Johnston:

> *"My irregular course of life had much imparied my health, for the re-establishment of which, and to enable me to pursue my studies without interruption from my free-living companions, my uncle advised my spending the approaching summer in York Town. Mr. Samuel Johnston, the Prothonotary of that county was his particular friend, a respectable man who had been in the practice of the law, and had a very good library. Having been appraised of the project, he kindly offered me the use of his books, as well as his countenance and assistance in my reading. . . . . It was in the spring of 1773 that I was transferred to this pleasant and flourishing village, situated above twelve miles beyond the Susquehanna . . . . . . I was well received by Mr. Johnston, but with that formal, theoretical kind of politeness, which distinguishes the manners of those who constitute the 'better sort', in small, secluded towns; and if, in these days, the Prothonotary of a county of German population, was not confessedly the most considerable personage in it, he must have been egregiously wanting to himself. This could with no propriety be imputed to my patron. Although apparently a mild and modest man, he evidently knew his consequence, and never lost sight of it, though to say the truth, I received full as much of his attention as either I desired or had a right to expect; He repeated the tender of his books and services, complimented me with a dinner, suggested that business and pleasure could not be well prosecuted together, and consigned me to my meditations."*

Much more to the liking of this light-hearted and sophisticated young man was the genial James Smith of whom he wrote with engaging candor:

> *"Besides my fellow boarders there was several young men in the town whose company served to relieve the dreariness of my solitude . . . . . There was also in the place an oddity, who, though not to be classed with its young men, I sometimes fell in with. This was Mr. James Smith, the lawyer, then in considerable practice. He was probably between forty and fifty years of age, fond of his bottle and young company, and possessed of an original species of drollery. This, as may perhaps be said of all persons in this way, consisted more in the manner than the matter; for which reason it is scarcely possible to convey a just notion of it to the reader. In him it much depended on an uncounthness of gesture, a certain ludicrous*

cast of countenance, and a drawling more of utterance, which taken in conjunction with his eccentric ideas, produced an effect irresistibly comical; though on an analysis it would be difficult to decide whether the man or the saying most constituted the jest. The most trivial incident from his mouth was stamped with his originality, and in relating one evening how he had been disturbed in his office by a cow, he gave inconceivable zest to his narrative by telling how she thrust her nose into the door, and there 'roared like a Numidian lion.'''

Choosing Sides   That Samuel Johnston and James Smith were cast from different molds is evidenced by Graydon's amusing vignettes. But the fundamental difference between Johnston and the men he instructed lay in their political convictions and basic loyalties. Johnston was the King's man. His personal code of honour prohibited any violation of his oath of allegiance to the crown. It is, therefore, a striking historic irony that four of the men who had sought his patronage should become leaders of the cause he abhorred and take up arms against his Sovereign Majesty, King George III.

But such as the turn of events that, within a few months after Graydon's return to Philadelphia, this "Dean" of York lawyers and his fellow members of the County Bar found themselves on opposite sides of the conflict which was to immortalize the name of James Smith as a Signer of the Declaration of Independence, and honor Col. Thomas Hartley, Captain Henry Miller, Major John Clark and Col. David Grier (a pupil of James Smith) as military heroes.

Daniel Batwell, Episcopal Rector, whose parishoners objected to his prayers for the Royal Family and his involvement with loyalist espionage.

Although Johnston did not suffer any such violence as was visited on the Tory Rector, Daniel Batwell, who was "dunked" in the Codorus and imprisoned for his views, his loyalty to the Crown cost him his post as Prothonotary, forced him to sell his property and move to Maryland, where, after the war, and in the face of strong opposition by the Attorney General, Luther Martin he was finally permitted to resume his practice of law.

By 1774 the coerceive acts of Parliment, passed in retaliation for the Boston Tea Party, had revoked the Charter of Massachusetts, closed the port of Boston and quartered General Gage with four regiments of British troops within that city. These punitive measures were so drastic as to evoke the comment from King George: "The die is now cast; the colonies must either submit or triumph."

But submission was not in their nature. Boston's appeal to the "Sister Colonies" to unite in a total boycott of English goods in order that she might not suffer alone for the common cause of liberty triggered their growing resentment into unified resistance.

For the patriots of York County the court house became the "Theater of Operations" for organizing their support of consolidated action to obtain redress of these tyrannies and to restore the liberties of British America. It was in the court house that the people assembled to elect James Smith, Joseph Donaldson and Thomas Hartley as their delegates to the Provincial Conference in Philadelphia and to organize a Committee of Safety composed of one or more representatives from each township. This Committee, with James Smith—President, Thomas Hartley—Vice President, John Hay—Treasurer, and George Leffler—Secretary, met regularly in the court house to carry out the recommendations of the Philadelphia Conference and of the First Continental Congress which met in Carpenter's Hall on September 5, 1774. The Court House was the forum for discussions on ways and means to assist the poor people of Boston, how best to enforce the non-importation of English goods, how to increase and conserve such vital supplies as wool, metals, saltpeter and gunpowder and methods of encouraging the development of military organizations already under way.

The temper of the people in York County, despite the numerous religious sects opposed to violence in any form, was inclined more to rebellion that to resistance. Such ties as bound many English colonists, especially the gentry, to the Mother Country did not exist for the German

A Forum of Freedom

39

and Scotch-Irish settlers who, for the most part, had originally fled from European oppression in favor of the more liberal government offered by the Penns. But the failure of the provincial government to provide any form of assistance . . . troops, munitions, supplies, or reimbursement for loss of life and property during the French and Indian War still rankled. This deep resentment coupled with the indignation aroused by the annexation of lands west of the mountains to Britain's new province of Quebec, after the peace of 1763, contributed significantly to the climate of revolt.

Time for Action   James Smith was one of the earliest proponents of armed resistance in the Province. Immediately upon his return from the first Philadelphia Conference, even before the organization of Continental Congress, he proceeded to organize the first military company in Pennsylvania for opposing British oppression. With Smith as Captain, Thomas Hartley First Lieutenant, David Grier Second Lieutenant, and Henry Miller Ensign, this company was equipped with rifles and met regularly for drill and instruction. When similar military groups known as "Associators" were formed throughout the County, James Smith, speaking in the Court House to the Committee of Correspondence, voiced his encouragement:

"We are of the opinion that said Associators, if trained with prudence, moderation and a strict regard to good order, under the direction of a man of probity and understanding, would tend much to the security of this country against the attempts of our enemies."

And he was right. The increasing show of arms and display of military skill strengthened the resolve of the citizen committees working to support the Cause, and their decisive actions, in turn, quickened the revolutionary spirit which was rapidly spreading among the people.

The letter which accompanied York County's donation of 246 pounds, 6 shillings, 10 pence to the improverished people of Boston in April of 1775 was, in itself, a pledge of support:

> *"Sorry are we to hear that the hand of oppression still bears hard on your city and that the distresses of your people are not yet alleviated. If your misfortunes and sufferings could be divided, the inhabitants of this county would cheerfully bear a part. This, it seems, cannot be done; your destined town must stand the shock alone. We want words to express the high sense we have of your conduct and virtue; few men in the world have opposed despotism and stood the torrent of ministerial vengeance with so much steadiness, intrepidity and resolution as the inhabitants of your town and country have done.*

You have true notions of liberty. You have purchased it. You ought to enjoy it. The noble stand made by the Massachusetts Bay, if faithfully adhered to, has laid the foundation of establishing American liberty on the most firm basis. The other colonies will be equal gainers by a favorable termination of the conquest and will not desert you in time of danger; they will doubtless grant you the most effectual assistance.''

But Boston was soon to receive assistance of a very different sort. ''The shot heard round the world'' (Concord, Massachusetts, April 19, 1775) had violent repercussions in the court house at York Town. Such was the state of preparedness in York County that when Congress issued a call for expert riflemen from Pennsylvania, Maryland and Virginia (June 14, 1775) the response was prompt and enthusiastic. Within two weeks after the Committee of Safety had received the word, a full company of volunteers had signed the required enlistment form as drafted by Congress:

''Military power will never awe a sensible American tamely to surrender his liberty.''

Samuel Adams

''I have this day voluntarily enlisted myself as a soldier in the American Continental Army for one year, unless sooner discharged, and do bind myself to conform in all instances to such rules and regulations as are, or shall be established for the government of said army.''

These first recruits, every one a skilled marksman, assembled in York, and, as was the custom, elected their officers: Michael Doudel, Captain... Henry Miller, First Lieutenant... John Dill, Second Lieutenant... James Matson, Third Lieutenant, and Walter Cruise, Corporal.

By the end of the month, thanks to the efficiency of the committee, and the resources of the men themselves, the company was fully equipped (''without a farthing being advanced from the Continental treasury'') and ready to begin their 400 mile march to Massachusetts. By the time General Washington arrived in Cambridge, July 2, 1775, to take command of the Continental army, the York troops were on their way.

Marching Orders

In the York Moravian Congregational Diary Pastor Neisser made the following entry (in German) for July 1, 1775:

''This afternoon a company of 100 men, of this town, left for the American army in New England, with the ringing of bells, after a sermom had been preached to them by the Presbyterian minister on the text. 1st Samuel x, 12, in which they were exhorted to keep God before their eyes during their expedition, and then they would be assured of His protection, otherwise this would not be the case.''

Traveling with amazing speed, Captain Doudel and his command

reached their destination about one o'clock on the afternoon of July 25th, the first company west and south of the Hudson to arrive on the scene where they were later assigned, together with eight other companies, to Colonel William Thompson's famous Regiment of Pennsylvania Riflemen.

To General Washington these frontier fighting men in their backwoods hunting shirts and Indian moccasins were brothers in arms. He had marched with them and camped with them. He knew their undisciplined loyalty, their uncanny marksmanship and their battle tactics. He had seen them fight from ambush, and had watched them stalk and kill the enemy as they stalked and killed the deer in their native forests. But to the British Regulars the Pennsylvania Riflemen were a new and awesome breed. Officers and men, who survived their fire, spread rumors of their prowess with a strange and deadly weapon, far more accurate and effective than their own smooth-bore muskets. The long, slim Pennsylvania rifle, with its incredible range of 250 yards, became a legend. Even General Howe wrote home about "the terrible guns of the rebels." A special reward was offered for the capture of these riflemen and their weapons, to be transported to England that the people might be moved to greater efforts against such savage foes.

One such captive was Corporal Walter Cruise of the York Company. Although his presence in London did little or nothing to stimulate recruitment, his trial and imprisonment caught the attention of Arthur Lee, the secret Ambassador of Congress in Britain. Lee managed to contact Cruise after his release from custody, arranged his transportation to Halifax, and entrusted him with a confidential report to Washington. The papers, which Cruise duly delivered to the Commander-in-Chief, warned him to prepare for a longer war than had been anticipated, and also carried the news that the King was hiring Hessian mercenaries to be included among the next reinforcements.

York had good reason to be proud of her fighting sons. Their regimental flag, bears the motto DOMARI NOLO. These fighting words, "I WILL NOT BE SUBJUGATED", symbolize the resolve and determination of York County as a whole, as well as the spirit and courage of Thompson's Battalion. A letter to Congress from the York Committee of Correspondence in July of 1775 gave voice to those sentiments:

> *"This spirit of the people on this occasion gave the committee encouragement. The men seemed actuated with the greatest zeal and thought*

themselves honored in having their names enrolled among the sons of liberty who are to fight for their country and in defense of their dearest rights and privileges. The only uneasiness they feel is that they are not this moment at the scene of action. From the spirit of the soldiers we entertain the most flattering hopes that they will prove serviceable to the cause of liberty and reflect honor on this county. The principal people here have caught the spirit of the honorable Congress and in their small circle have done everything in their power to animate their neighbors to stand forth in this day of despotism and resist the arbitrary and unjust measures of Parliament with all the power which heaven has given them. And we have the pleasure to inform you that their labors have not been in vain and that the county is ready to strain every nerve to put into execution any measures which the Congress may judge necessary to our common defense.''

York Countians were not given to false promises. As the war escalated so did their supportive action. On July 28th and 29th the court house was the scene of joint meetings of the Committee of Safety and the Officers of the Associators at which the county was divided into five military districts, each one to raise its own battalion. At these same sessions a Battalion (5 companies) of Minute Men was also organized to be ready on short warning to take to the field.

More and more farmers exchanged the plow for the sword, the hay fork for the rifle and bayonet. Between 1775 and 1783 it is estimated that 4,000 men from York County were under arms and participated in every major engagement of the war.

For July 7, 1776 Pastor Neisser wrote in the Moravian Diary: ''Strict orders came that all ''Associators'' of this county should hold themselves in readiness to march to the front. In the following week they left.''

''The Front'', at that time was Trenton and New Brunswick in New Jersey.

The next entry, July 17, pictures conditions at York Town and the concern of a congregation torn between loyalty to country and adherence to religious opposition to violence:

Deserted Village

''York Town seems quite deserted on account of the departure of all men under fifty years of age. Our young men had to leave for the army in Jersey. Christian Heckedorn and William Lanius have, after a great deal of trouble, succeeded in preventing themselves from being taken along, on account of their sickness. Jacob Rothrock has also escaped being drafted. But Ernst Schlosser, the three sons of Bro. Rothrock, Brinkman, John

Seifer's eldest son, John Hoenrison, and, in short, the most of the others who are under fifty years of age, will have to march off in the next few days. Thus only the old brethren and sisters will be left. Several of our people, because the town has been so emptied, have, in addition to several other persons, been elected as members of the Committee ad interim, with a guard given them day and night, in order to maintain peace and order, and give security against the plots of the Tories. All business and every occupation are prostrate, all shops are closed. How many prayers and tears will now be brought before the Lord, by parents for their children, by children for their parents, by wives for their husbands."

Support and Supplies In addition to supplying troops for Washington's hard-pressed army, York County also furnished a large and varied quantity of supplies. In 1775 the York County Committee of Safety authorized the shipment of 49 quarter casks of gunpowder, 3,770 pounds of lead as well as arms and equipment to the Pennsylvania Council of Safety and similar shipments were made to outlying counties. Guns, powder, and ammunition, lead, hand-forged swords, gun flints, corn, flour, hay, oats, rye, whiskey, shingles, nails, tar and tar pots, ropes, blankets, horses, saddles, barrels of beer and pork, bar iron and cannon balls from county forges... all of these vital materials helped keep the armies on the move. York craftsmen also played an important defense role as the services of gunsmiths, tinsmiths, wagonmakers, blacksmiths, tanners, saddlers and coopers were in great demand.

During these years the court house remained the hub of activity, the nerve center of communication with Congress and with the new General Assembly which, after the Constitutional Convention of 1776 and the dissolution of the Provincial government, became the governing body of the state. Here dispatches arrived from Philadelphia, and from the other colonies relating to the decisions of Congress and the progress of the war. It was from Court House Square the people learned of Washington's success in driving the British out of Boston, the failure of the American expedition in Canada, the arrival of Hessian mercenaries, the capture of 400 York County Troops at Fort Washington in the unsuccessful defense of New York, Washington's retreat through New Jersey and his victories at Trenton and Princeton, offset by Howe's unexpected landing at the head of the Chesapeake, and Washington's defeat at the bloody Brandywine, followed two weeks later by the British occupation of Philadelphia.

On September 27, 1777 a courier brought the most electrifying news of all — Congress was on its way to York! Less than 15 months after signing the Declaration of Independence, 25 of the men who had pledged their "lives, their fortunes and their sacred honor" to its support would be meeting with other delegates in the unpretentious court house at York Town where their decisions would determine the destiny of a new society, already conceived, but not yet brought forth as a united political entity. The story of the dramatic and far-reaching events which transpired here between September 30th, 1777 and June 27th, 1778 is essentially the story of "The Birth of a Nation."

Davis Gray watercolor

Courtesy of The York Bank and Trust Company

Voices of Fear and Determination

At six o'clock on Friday morning, September 12, 1777, John Hancock summoned the members of the Second Continental Congress to acquaint them with Washington's report of his defeat in the previous day's battle at Brandywine and his retreat to Chester. At five o'clock of the same day that body "Resolved that the commissary general of purchases be directed to purchase, on the most reasonable terms he can, 30 hogsheads of rum, and that the same be presented to the army, and distributed among the soldiers, in such manner as the General shall direct, in compliment to the soldiers for their gallant behavior in the late battle with the enemy."

By this thoughtful gesture the men whose lives were surely forfeit, should Philadelphia fall into British hands, showed their true mettle in the face of imminent disaster. With careful deliberation, but without panic, they prepared for the worst. Washington was directed to give the necessary orders for "completing the defenses of the Delaware River."

On Sunday, September 14th, the Supreme Executive Council of Pennsylvania was asked to "appoint proper and discreet persons to take into possession any linens, blankets and other woolens, shoes, spirits, and other necessaries for the use of the army which they, may find in any stores or warehouses in the city of Philadelphia, giving a certificate expressing the quantity and value, and to cause the goods so taken to be conveyed to some secure place." At this same session arrangements were also made "to remove all public bells in Philadelphia to a place of security, upon a near approach of the enemy." Pertaining to their personal safety, the Journal for

Preparations for Flight

that date records: "That if Congress shall be obliged to remove from Philadelphia, Lancaster shall be the place at which they shall meet."

Papers more precious than People

But much more specific instructions were given for the protection of the documents whose safety was regarded more highly than their own. "Resolved that the public papers be put under the care of Mr. (Abraham) Clark, and that he be empowered, upon the Congress removing to Lancaster, to procure wagons sufficient for conveying them thither, and apply to General Dickinson, or any other officer commanding troops in the army of the United States, who is hereby directed to furnish a guard to conduct the said papers safe to Lancaster."

Every day that Congress remained in the city increased their danger, but there was much to be done. General Washington requested that the provisions in the city be removed to a place of safety, reserving only what would be necessary for the inhabitants and for the army under his command. By September 17th time was running out. Admittedly, "the city of Philadelphia, notwithstanding the brave exertions of the American army, might possibly be for a time possessed by the enemy's army", and that for the public welfare, Congress might have to adjourn to some place more remote from the scene of action where they could continue their deliberations without interruption. Therefore, for a period of 60 days, Washington was given carte blanche to confiscate any and all goods and provisions necessary to the subsistence of his army or of service to the enemy, within a 70 mile circumference of his headquarters.

The Warning

The next day Congress took the further precaution of ordering Major General Armstrong to remove all printing presses and types (save one) to secure places in the country. The Journal for September 18th concluded with the usual entry: "Adjourned to 10 o'Clock tomorrow."

But during the night their plans were changed. A warning from Col. Alexander Hamilton that the British were about to cross the Schuylkill River precipitated their departure. Accounts of their leave-taking are many and varied.

Rivington's Gazette, a Tory paper, carried the colorful but highly inaccurate story:

"As soon as the rebels learned that the British fleet was at the head of the Chesapeake, a motion was made in Congress for an adjournment to some place 'at least one hundred miles from any part of God's Kingdom where the British mercenaries can possibly land,' which, after some rapturous

demonstrations, was carried. Immediately the Congress commenced the retreat, leaving old nosey Thomson [Secretary of Congress] to pick up the duds and write promises to pay (When Congress should return) the Congress debts. In the flight, as in the rebellion, Hancock, having a just apprehension of the vengeance which awaits him, took the initiative and was the first to carry out the letter of the motion of his associates.''

A Tory teen-ager, Robert Morton, wrote in his diary that Hamilton's warning "so much alarmed the Gentlemen of the Congress, the military officers, and other friends to the general cause of American freedom and independence, that they decamped with the utmost precipitation, and in the greatest confusion, insomuch that one of the delegates, by name (Nathaniel) Fulsom (of New Hampshire) was obliged in a very fulsom manner to ride off without a saddle!''

More personal and less dramatic accounts are to be found in the correspondence of individual members. Thomas Burke wrote to Governor Caswell of North Carolina as follows:

*Nathanial Folsum
1726-1790
New Hampshire Delegate*

> *"The question of adjournment from Philadelphia was daily agitated in congress but always overruled. On the night before last we received a complete decision. Intelligence was received from the General officer commanding on Schuylkill that the Enemy were then attempting to cross, and that they could not be prevented, and advising the congress immediately to remove from the city. The movement was made, not by vote, but by universal consent for every member consulted his own particular safety. I was awakened by a servant about 2 A.M. and though I lost no time preparing to depart, yet I did not choose to retreat with precipitation. I was not, indeed, fully persuaded of the necessity of the measure, and not very apprehensive for my personal safety."*

Henry Laurens of South Carolina, whose counsel for organized evacuation plans had been ignored by Congress, described his own departure in a letter to the American General, Robert Howe, as even more deliberate:

> *"I had sent forward my baggage followed it that Evening and next Morning, after many thousands had passed by me, I made my breakfast, filled my pipe, and soberly entered my carriage, drove gently on to Bristol, took in the wounded Marquis de Lafayette (wounded at Brandywine) and proceeded to Bethlehem, thence to Reading and Lancaster. Here Congress were soon convened, but hearts were still fluttering in some bosoms and a motion made for adjourning to this town. (York)"*

John Adams, having previously warned his beloved Abigail against undue anxiety for himself or the ''great and sacred cause'' should Philadelphia be taken, wrote in his Diary for September 19th:

> *"At three this morning was waked by Mr. Lovel, and told that the members of Congress were gone, some of them, a little after midnight, that there was a letter from Mr. Hamilton, aid-de-camp to the General, informing that the enemy were in possession of the ford and the boats, and had it in their power to be in Philadelphia before morning, and that, if Congress was not removed, they had not a moment to lose. Mr. Marchant and myself arose, sent for our horses, and after collecting our things, rode off after the others. Breakfasted at Bristol, where were many members determined to go the Newton road to Reading. We rode to Trenton, where we dined. Col. Harrison, Dr. Witherspoon, all the delegates from New York and New England, except Gerry and Lovel."*

The whereabouts of the missing Mr. James Lovell are explained in his letter to Joseph Trumbull, Governor of Connecticut, dated September 23rd.

Philada, 23rd Sept. (1777)

> *"Mr dear Sir:*
>
> *You will have heard before this reaches you that Congress left this City at 3 oClock in the Morning of the 19th in Consequence of Advice by Express from Coll. A Hamilton, Washington's Aid-de-Camp whose Horse was shot as he was passing the Schuylkill and one also of his Oarsman was killed. I know not which way Coll. Dyer and Co. steered after they crossed into the Jersies. I was averse to going at first, and after breakfasting at Bristol, Curiosity and some Interest brought me back here to dine the same day. It is said that 4,000 of the Enemy have now actually crossed at Swede's Ford. I shall know the Truth before the Post goes off Tomorrow."*

Unhappily for Mr. Lovell, his curiosity cost him his pocketbook, stolen ''in the Twinkling of an Eye last fryday Eveng. at the Coffee-House, containing 260 Dollars with 15 or more Lottery Tickets belonging to Col. Whipple and some papers'' of his own. However, he remained in Philadelphia until the 25th when ''the Enemy being within a mile and without any opposing Troops in the city,'' he ''slipt into the Jersies.'' ''It was lucky'', as he recalled later, ''that I had a young Lady to gallant thither; for 3 or 4 Officers who left Philida before me, were taken in the Franckfort Road.''

It was, indeed, lucky for all concerned that no members of Congress were captured en route. They traveled, not as a body, but singly or in small groups of their own friends, and by whatever means of transportation they could command on short notice. Most of them made the journey on horseback. President Hancock used a carriage and Joseph Jones of Virginia arrived in a coach he had previously borrowed from General Washington. The vehicle was, apparently, somewhat the worse for wear, as indicated in a note from the borrower to the lender.

> *"The bolt that fastens the pole part of the long reins was lost, some brass nails also gone, and the lining much dirtied and in some places torn. I will have these little matters repaired and the carriage and harness dept clean and in as good order as I can, which is the least I can do for the use thereof."*

The circuitous route deemed necessary for the protection of state papers "of more importance than all the members" led from Philadelphia to Bristol, on to Trenton, back into Pennsylvania via Easton, Bethlehem and Reading and thence to Lancaster, a total distance of 180 miles. Although a few members had arrived as early as the 24th of September, it was not until the 27th that Congress convened its first and only meeting in Lancaster, a session at which the following resolution was adopted:

The Road to York Town

> *"That the Treasury Board direct the treasurer, with all his papers, forms, &c. to repair to the town of York, in Pennsylvania.*
> *Adjourned to York-Town, there to meet on Tuesday next at 10 o'Clock."*

The sentiments expressed in the foregoing excerpts from letters and diaries clearly show that the men who finally assembled in the Court House at York Town were not the fear-ridden refugees of Tory description, but rather a philosophical band of temporary exiles determined on "business as usual." Nor were they unduly alarmed by the fall of Philadelphia. The year before, when the Government had fled to Baltimore for two months (December 20 — February 27, 1776) they had agreed with Washington that its capture "must prove of the most fatal consequences to the cause of America." But this time, having removed themselves and their documents beyond Howe's immediate reach, and having stripped the city of its stores, they could afford to play a waiting game. Philadelphia was not a supply center and Washington's army was receiving reinforcements from Virginia, Maryland, New York and New Jersey. As John Adams put it: "If Howe gets the city, it will cost him all his forces to keep it, and so he can get nothing else." Benjamin Franklin's reaction when he heard the news in Paris, was of the same tenor: "Howe captured Philadelphia? No! Philadelphia has captured Howe!"

Haven for Exiles   From all indications, the decision that "The Susquehanna should flow between the Congress and the enemy" was born, not of panic, but of common sense. The little town on the far side of the river was not unknown to Congress. On July 5, 1776 it was "Resolved that the British officers and soldiers who are prisoners and now in New Jersey be sent from thence to the town of York, in Pennsylvania." Later, on December 13th of the same year, it was resolved that a magazine be formed at York, Pennsylvania and another at Springfield, Massachusetts. Although this resolution was superceded by one on December 27th placing the magazine at Carlisle, the point of recognition remains the same. Also, on February 15, 1777 York Town was named the convention site for commissioners from New York, New Jersey, Pennsylvania, Delaware, Maryland and Virginia who met on March 26th to recommend methods of price control on labor, goods and materials to their various legislatures.

Furthermore, two of the Pennsylvania delegates possessed first-hand knowledge of the town and its people. To James Smith, himself a signer of the Declaration and, therefore as mindful of his safety as the next man, Yorkers had proven their patriotism many times over. He understood the Pennsylvania Germans, appreciated their support, and respected the beliefs of the non-militant sects which posed no threat of betrayal. He was well aware of the general hostility toward loyalist sympathizers, expressed in some instances by imprisonment or the tar and feather treatment. Smith was also in an excellent position to assess and organize the facilities necessary for the accommodation of his fellow congressmen.

Daniel Roberdeau, a Philadelphia merchant and former member of the Pennsylvania Assembly, had served with York Countian James Ewing, as a Brigadier of the Flying Camp in 1776 and could vouch for the valor of York troops. He had also been chosen a member of the Council of Safety from whom York had received the following commendation:

"The spirited and firm behavior of the inhabitants of York County in support of the righteous cause in which America is embarked, has the full approbation of the Committee of Safety and merits their just esteem."

Although not an actual resident, Roberdeau had been sufficiently attracted to York as to become a property owner and tax-payer. On March 4th, shortly before taking his seat in Congress, he had purchased a dwelling from Michael and Margaret Doudel, located on the north side of Market Street, west of the Codorus.

The adjournment of Congress to York on September 27th was neither as sudden or as unexpected as it seemed. On September 14th John Adams had mentioned that York was among the Pennsylvania towns being considered as a possible retreat, and on September 24th James Lovell had written to Elbridge Gerry: "By all I can find, you will be so sick of Lancaster as to determine upon York speedily."

It was, therefore, not merely York's geographical location, but the quality of the town itself which offered them the security and support they so sorely needed. Here, at least, according to the appraisal of delegates James Duane from New York, they would be "sufficiently retired" that they could deliberate without fear of interruption."

To a government in exile no situation is ideal. The men who crossed the Susquehanna into York County were fatigued and frustrated. They were disgruntled by their unceremonious and hasty departure from Philadelphia, and, no doubt, secretly disquieted by the memory of Franklin's famous admonition, "We must all hang together, or, most assuredly we will all hang separately."

The current Tory-based rumor, rife in Philadelphia since January first, that 1777 would be the "year of the Hangman" did not add to their peace of mind. To men with a price on their heads, each of those three 7's on the calendar bore a striking and grim resemblance to the gallows-tree.

Voices In Exile

The Lamentations of Congress

The Court House was far from crowded on the Tuesday morning of September 30th, when John Hancock took his seat on the Justices' Bench to preside over the first York session of Continental Congress. Only five of the hastily assembled tables and chairs were in use as most of the delegates were still en route. Charles Thomson, the faithful secretary who served for 15 years without missing a session, was in his place, but the Journal entry for that day was one of the shortest on record: "Met and adjourned to 10 o'Clock tomorrow."

The next day, with 25 members present and accounted for, a proper business meeting was conducted at which the following work schedule was adopted:

> "Ordered, that until further order, Congress shall meet at ten o'Clock A.M. sit to one, then adjourn to four P.M. then to meet and proceed on business."

With committee meetings lasting far into the evening hours, the members of Congress would have been well served had there been living quarters within the building itself, since that was where they spend most of their time. As it was, a town of 1800 inhabitants and less than 300 houses most of them, with a few exceptions, small log structures of primitive design and simple furnishings, could offer little in the way of comfort, and nothing that could approximate luxury. The dozen or more Publick Houses were adequate as stop-overs for wagoners and travelers, but hardly equipped to accommodate resident guests. Furthermore, the town was already more crowded than usual with people who had fled their homes in the Philadelphia area to seek shelter with relatives and friends.

Nevertheless, in one way or another, some provision had to be made for the delegates and their servants, the employees of Congress, the troops who had guarded the transfer of their priceless papers, members of the Board of War and the Treasury. Naturally, accommodations near the Court House were at a premium. James Smith offered his South George Street law office (the very one in which the cow had "roared like a Numidian lion") as headquarters for the Board of War and the Committee on Foreign Affairs. Another distinguished patriot, Archibald McLean, opened his house in the north east quadrant of the Square to the Treasury under Chairman Elbridge Gerry and Treasurer, Michael Hillegas. President John Hancock found lodgings at the home of Mrs. Eva Swope whose husband, Col. Michael Swope, commander of the York troops at Fort Washington, was being held as a prisoner of war in New York. This dwelling, conveniently located three doors west of the Square on Market Street, was henceforth known as "The President's House."

One of the Pennsylvania delegates, General Daniel Roberdeau, the wealthy and generous Philadelphia merchant who had turned over his privateer prize money of $22,000 to the Treasury, rented a property at the south west corner of the Square, facing on George Street, where he installed his children and his two sisters. In this spacious two and one half story dwelling, said to be the largest in town, John and Samuel Adams, Elbridge Gerry, Benjamin Harrison and Richard Henry Lee enjoyed a warmth and hospitality not to be found anywhere else. However, it is interesting to note that Edward Langworthy of Georgia experienced a different kind of hospitality at the inn of Elizabeth Moore, where he met and courted a daughter of the house. The marriage bond of Langworthy and Mary Moore is dated July 23, 1778.

The local tradition that Thomas Paine, the great pamphleteer, lodged at the Cookes House, while serving in York as Secretary of the Committee on Foreign Affairs, has long been debated. Located about a mile south west of the Square, the old stone house was built in 1761. There are records to show that some congressmen stabled their horses on the premises, but none to substantiate the legend of Paine's occupancy. That Paine was actually in residence at York is clearly authenticated in his leter to Franklin, datelined YORK, MAY 16, 1778:

"After October 23, I returned to Col. Kirkbridge's (Lancaster) where I stayed a fortnight until the latter end of January, 1778. After that I went to York and Published (addressed) Crisis No. 5 to General Howe. I have begun No. 6 which I intend to address to Lord North."

The foregoing passage leaves no doubt that Paine lived and worked in York from the end of January to mid-May. But WHERE?

Another puzzling question pertains to the whereabouts of the Declaration of Independence while Congress was in York. It must certainly have been among the state papers hauled "from Lancaster to Reading and thence York Town" for which Congress paid "waggon hire" of sixteen dollars on November 28th.

But there is no mention of its custody. Secretary Thomson might have had it in his keeping, wherever his lodgings may have been, but the more general and more logical assumption is that it remained under lock and key in the Court House itself. The sum of $32.00 paid to Jacob Funk, a local carpenter for making "two boxes with locks and a large chest for the Secretary's office" may or may not have some bearing on the matter.

The Chaplains of Congress, the Rev. William White and the Rev.

George Duffield, were housed, as might be expected, with local clergy-men — the former at the Christ Lutheran parsonage on North George Street, then occupied by Pastor John Nicholas Kurtz, the latter with the Rev. Daniel Wagner of Zion Reformed Church residing on East King Street.

Episcopal clergy faced the difficult task of eliminating prayers for the King to whom they were bound by oaths of allegiance, but voted to do so July 4, 1776. Bishop White of Christ Church, Philadelphia, was a frequent and well loved visitor to York in his later years.

Lithographed silhouette by Brown

Bishop William White, 1748-1836, Chaplin to Congress

It is too much to hope that history will ever pinpoint the precise habitations of the sixty four delegates who came and went during the nine months Congress sat in York Town. No official records were kept, and it is only from mention made in their diaries and correspondence that such details come to light. For example, Dr. Josiah Bartlett of New Hampshire wrote: "I now put up at one Hoffman's on the west side of the Bridge, quite at the west end of town, at a German house where I am obliged to be German in most respects."

Thomas McKean of Delaware reported that he lived "in a little dutch tavern, at an enormous expense for ten days" before he could get other lodgings.

Elias Boudinot of New Jersey summed up the housing situation in his description of York as a "well built town about the size of Reading", but "as full as a tick!"

This scarcity of lodgings, "frequently attended by bad fare", and the inflationary prices constituted a real hardship for men of limited means. All of the delegates, with the exception of the President, whose accounts came out of government funds, were paying their own expenses, and the cost of living was rapidly exceeding the stipends of five to eight dollars a day allotted by their individual states. However, inflation, that "canker of civilian morale", did not originate in York. For months Congress had been struggling unsuccessfully with price controls and the devaluation of Continental currency. Early in February Thomas Burke had written:

> "if we go on emitting money, the quantity in circulation so enhances the price of things that we shall only make money without being able to get for it more commodities, and it will, of course, destroy its own purpose."

Before departing from Philadelphia the thrifty John Adams had recorded prices as double or triple those of 1776 . . . 4 pounds a week for board . . . Shoes, five dollars a pair . . . Salt, $27 a bushel . . . Butter, 10 shillings a pound . . . Punch, 20 shillings a Bowl. At the time he was lamenting that never in his life had he lived so meanly and poorly.

Small wonder, then, that the correspondence of delegates meeting in York should bear so many references to this universal problem.

Jonathan Elmer of New Jersey managed to keep himself and one horse for seven weeks at a cost of sixty five pounds, roughly $175. But Oliver Wolcott, who arrived from Connecticut with Samuel Huntingdom in February of 1778, when the town was even more crowded, estimated that "a single man exclusive of Horsekeeping cannot probably live under at least ten pounds per week", adding that "Everything here bears an enormous price."

Timothy Pickering, serving with the Board of War, wrote to his wife in Massachusetts that Congressmen were obliged to pay about $37 a week for board alone. Although Cornelius Harnett of North Carolina cut his costs to $200 for two months, he declared he had never lived in so wretched a manner in his whole life. As to the exhorbitant rates at Publick Houses, James Lovell made the caustic comment that "a Man must pay ten dollars for glancing at a Tavern, and ten or twelve shillings a night for his horse's gnawing the Rock."

By reason of paper money having dropped to about 34 cents on the dollar ("not worth a Continental") and their home treasuries being so far

"The horrid scene of extortion here is shocking . . . Is there no way to put a stop to these enormities?"
Danial Roberdeau

away, some congressmen simply could not make ends meet, and were forced to apply for government advances. Writing to Thomas Burke, a fellow-delegate on leave, Harnett regarded such necessity both as a personal embarrassment and as a danger signal of further economic distress:

> *"I shall be under the necessity of procuring in advance from the Treasury at least $1000 over and above my allowance from the state which is very handsome. I shall be content if this will bring me home with a single dollar in my pocket. Mention not this: if you do, I am sure you will not be believed, but it is as true as the Gospel. God only knows what this country will come to at last."*

Worried by finances, plagued by homesickness, exhausted by long hours of debate and paper work, and, above all, disappointed in the hope that Washington would speedily turn defeat into a victory which would permit their early return to Philadelphia, even the most patient members of Congress grew irritable. As is the wont of men on long enforced absences from home and family, whether in military or civilian service, they complained about any and everything in their immediate surroundings.

James Lovell vowed that the "lime water had torn many of his countrymen's bowels out and had forced some delegates home to their native springs". In November, Richard Henry Lee, who was then cutting his budget by a diet of roast wild pigeons purchased from farmers for a few cents a dozen, also blamed the ill state of his health on "bad water, air and excessive business."

Henry Laurens observed that his office and lodgings at York Town were not nearly so large as the hall of his Mt. Tacitus Plantation in North Carolina, and that more than once he was compelled to "dine on bread and cheese and a bit of grog!"

In late October, after "three days of soaking and poaching in the heaviest rain that has been known for several years", the testy Mr. Adams lost what little patience he had. Although admittedly more comfortable than most, in his lodgings with the genial and considerate Roberdeau, he none the less complained to Abigail:

> *"The house where I am is so thronged that I cannot enjoy such accommodations as I wish. I cannot have a room as I used, and therefore, cannot find opportunities to write as I once did."*

In the same letter he was so forgetful of York's loyalty, and generous support of Boston in his home state, as to lash out at the Pennsylvania Germans:

60

"The people of this country are chiefly Germans who have schools in their own language as well as prayers, Psalms and sermons, so that multitudes are born, grow up and die here without ever learning English. In politics they are a breed of mongrels or neutrals and benumbered with a general torpor."

Although these comments were no worse than his prior assessment of the Philadelphia Quakers, whom he termed "as dull as beetles . . . a kind of neutral tribe or the race of the insipids" . . . they were particularly ill-timed. Only two months before, Adams had shared in the decision of Congress that Col. Daniel Morgan and his riflemen be sent to the aid of the northern army. The Pennsylvania rifle, whose deadly accuracy was to spell victory at Saratoga, was certainly not the invention of a "mongrel" or "torpid" people. Had the Pennsylvania Germans made no other contribution to American independence, their place in history would have been well assured.

Such unflattering comments by members of Congress were to be more or less expected. During their previous flight to Baltimore, which James Lovell regarded as a "Trifle compared with the present Jaunt and Situation", that city was branded by Dr. Benjamin Rush as "The Damnedest Hole in the World." William Hooper of North Carolina, even more explicitly, declared that the Devil had marked "this delectable spot and reserved it for his own particular seat and inheritance." A page in the diary of John Adams recorded: "The weather was rainy, and the streets the muddiest I ever saw. This is the dirtiest place in the world."

It is not surprising, therefore, that the town of York, even less populated and less developed, would suffer its share of abuse. Although the court house itself escaped criticism, the grueling schedule of long hours and frustrating arguments generated a spirit of discontent, not only with the town, but with the whole body of Congress, and everything pertaining to it.

John Matthews begged Governor Rutledge of South Carolina for a leave of absence:

"I have wrote to you for leave to come home in December. For God's sake, procure it for me, and I'll be damned if you ever catch me here again. Those who have dispositions for Jangling, and are fond of displaying their Rhetorical abilities, let them come. I was never so sick of anything in my life."

Nathaniel Folsom sorely needed the support of Josiah Bartlett, his fellow-representative from New Hampshire:

"My Duty is Very hard, and if you have any Comepashon left for me hope you will Joyne Congress Soone, as the business is too much for one to live under."

Early in October Cornelius Harnett was feeling the pangs of homesickness:

"At present I can hardly find time to write a letter. Congress sits from morning 'till night, and Committees 'till 10 and 11 o'Clock. In fact, I am almost tired of my troublesome office, and heartily wish to be with my family."

The following month, with no relief in sight, he made a further appeal in the form of a post script to a letter to his friend, Thomas Burke:

"P.S. For God's sake, endeavor to get some gentlemen appointed in my stead. I cannot stay here any longer with any pleasure."

By the end of December his indignation was all-encompassing:

"Believe me it is the most inhospitable scandalous place I was ever in. If I can once more return to my family all the Devils in Hell shall not separate us. The honor of being once a member of Congress is sufficient for me. I acknowledge it is the highest honor a free state can bestow on one of its members. I shall be careful to ask for nothing more, but will sit under my own vine and my own Fig Tree (for I have them both) at Poplar Grove where none shall make me afraid except the boats of the British cruisers."

"If you inquire what the people are like here, I must answer — 'The same as anywhere.'"
Goethe

Although these criticisms, and others like them . . . "This York Town is a vile quarter" . . . "The people here are not obliging" . . . "The horrid scene of extortion is shocking" . . . cannot be interpreted as bona fide descriptions of the town (probably no better or worse than any other rural settlement of the era) they do serve to mirror the moods and manners of the men who voiced them. As Thomas Carlyle put it, "In every man's writings the character of the writer must lie recorded." The representatives of the thirteen original states assembled in the York Court House were the leaders and founders of a new nation, but they were not super-men. Subject to all the bodily ills and mental torments that flesh is heir to, they did the best they could under the most trying circumstances. In exchanging the amenities of the second largest city of the English speaking world for the safety of an unsophisticated village, Congress was faced with adjustments and concessions which some members were able to make with better grace than others. Not everyone had Thomas McKean's philosophy: "We must not

62

expect much comfort during this great and glorious struggle.'' And few possessed the adaptability of Timothy Pickering whose Valentine's Day letter to his wife shows how he and his servant, Millet, adjusted to the simple life style which must have been the pattern of an average York Town household:

York Town, February 14, 1778

'''Tis more difficult getting a habitation than I expected. I was puzzled to find a place to lodge at. Finally, I was led to the widow MIHMINS (the widow of a Dutch Physician.) But she said she had no bed but one, her own, nor could furnish me with diet. I told her I could find both. To this she consented to take me in. I am happy that she did, for she is a very neat, clever, obliging old woman, and has agreed to wash and mend my linen and stockings which is a great thing here. What her price will be I do not know, but I am sure not extravagant. The old lady often puts me in mind of my mother. She is in all respects kind and motherly. I have not felt so much at home since I left Salem. She lived all alone and now sets from morning till night at her spinning wheel, which, by the way, is a very modest one. And when I am at home writing or reading it gives me no more disturbance than the purring of a cat.

She has one decent lower room warmed by a stove after the German fashion. (She is of that nation.) and a small kitchen furnished with every utensil in pretty order. There she gets her own victuals and Millet cooks for me.

Besides the lower room and kitchen there is a warm chamber where I lodge. In one corner Millet has fixed me a little cabin in which he has put a straw bed, and upon that my mattress, a bag of straw makes my bolster and my pillow is upon that. I lie between my sheet doubled — the other sheet was stollen from me at Wilmington last September — my blanket lies double upon that and my great coat and other clothes over all. In this manner I have lain every night warm and comfortable. In another corner of the chamber Millet lies on a bed of chaff, furnished by the landlady. These chaff beds are very good. 'Tis the chaff of wheat and is much preferable to straw.

Millet has bought a tolerable veal at a shilling a pound, butter at two thirds of a dollar, eggs at one third of a dollar, a dozen and potatoes at a dollar a bushel. But above all he gets a quart of good milk every night and every morning which with good bread at a third of a dollar a loaf of about six pounds weight makes our breakfast and supper.

But half the time as we dine late we need no supper, so we have milk enough for good puddings. The milk costs me 12 pence a quart. At the next door Millet gets excellent beer of a brewer at half dollar a gallon. Thus my diet is perfectly agreeable. I have directed Millet to get some rice and Indian meal and when they are obtained, I shall want for nothing.

This little detail I thought would no more than satisfy your curiosity. At the same time, I suppose it may divert you and your friends. I confess, notwithstanding all I have said, that I have my doubts about the expediency of you coming this way as soon as I at first proposed. I say so soon because, if we regain Philadelphia in the course of the next campaign — which I trust we shall — and all things get quiet here, and I am likely to continue at the Board of War, I shall then most certainly determine to bring you away from Salem and not pass another winter without you.''

This bit of personal correspondence, with its good-humored overtones of warmth and friendship, somewhat off-sets the general impression of resentment and hostility created by previous quotes. Pickering's attempt to give his German landlady's name a Holland spelling, ''M-I-H-M-I-N-S, is typical of the common confusion between the words ''Dutch'' and ''Deutsch''. The widow of a Dutch Physician'' was most likely the widow of JOHN MEEM, familiarly known in the community as ''Doctor'' or ''Doc''. Meem was one of the carpenters employed by the County Commissioners for the building of the court house, and his property, Lot #124, on the South East corner of Market and Pershing Avenue, might well have been that in which Pickering felt himself so much at home.

But regardless of where or how these public servants lived, all roads led to the Court House. Here, in the first few weeks of their exile, they learned of Washington's defeat at Germantown, and received the news of the defection of their first official chaplain, the Rev. Jacob Duché. The Philadelphia rector, after one day as a British captive, had betrayed the cause for which, in 1774, he had prayed "with such fervency, purity, and solemnity, of style and sentiment that even the Quakers shed tears."

Duché's duplicity took the form of an impassioned letter to Washington begging that he advise Congress to rescind "the hasty and ill-advised declaration of independency", "to order an immediate cessation of hostilities", or, should Congress refuse, "Negotiate for America at the head of your army." Washington's immediate reaction was to forward this letter to Congress which was deeply affected, not only by its treasonable intent, but by the scathing comments directed against individual members.

Imagine the indignation of such proud Virginians as Francis Lightfoot and Richard Henry Lee described as "men whose minds can never mingle with your own", the wrath of the Pennsylvania delegates "some so obscure their names have never met my ears before — others only distinguished for the weakness of their understandings and the violence of their tempers." The tempers of the New Englanders must have boiled over at Duché's rhetorical question:

> "From the New England provinces can you find one that, as a gentlemen you could wish to associate with, unless the soft and mild address of Mr. Hancock can atone for the want of every other qualification necessary for the seat he fills? Bankrupts, attorneys, and men of desperate fortunes are his colleagues."

John Adams dismissed the whole affair with the comment: "Poor man! I pity his weakness and detest his wickedness." Nathaniel Folsom wrote a stronger report to his friend, Josiah Bartlett, one of the signers of that "hasty and ill-advised declaration:"

> "I inclose you a Coppey of a letter from the Revt. mr. Ducha to general Washington that you may See what a Judas wase a Chaplin to Congress. would not have you make it Public unless it be by advice of Councile, as Congress have not thought fit to Publish it here, tho it is Publick anough in everybody's mouth in the Streets."

Duché's failure to corrupt Washington cost him the confidence of the

Loyalist Snobbery

"Q. What kind of men compose Congress?
A. It consists of obscure, pettifogging attorneys, bankrupt shopkeepers, outlawed smugglers, etc., etc."
a Loyalist Catechism

British, although he received an "A for Effort" reward of sorts by being appointed Chaplain to The Asylum for Female Orphans at Lambeth during his residence in England. This unhappy man, whose goods and property had been confiscated by Pennsylvania, was permitted to return to Philadelphia in 1792, where it is reported, he was courteously received by the President of the United States, the incorruptible and magnanimous George Washington.

A similar case to come before Congress was that of the Rev. Daniel Batwell, York's Tory rector whose "dunking in the Codorus", as previously mentioned, was followed by arrest and imprisonment. The Journal of Congress for the four o'clock session of October 2nd records the following action:

> *"The petition of the Rev. Mr. Daniel Batwell, setting forth, that, on a charge of being concerned in a conspiracy to destroy the continental magazines in this State, he was in custody of the keeper of the gaol of York County, by virtue of a committment, until Congress or the supreme executive council of this State should take further order touching him, or until he should be otherwise discharged according to law, being presented to Congress and read; and it appearing to Congress, by the certificate of Dr. Jameson that the petitioner is so much emaciated, by a complication of disorders, that his life will be endangered, unless removed from the said gaol:*

> *RESOLVED, That the said petition be referred to the president and supreme executive council of this State, to take such order relative to the petitioner as they shall think proper; and that, in the mean time, the keeper of the gaol be directed to remove the petitioner to some other safe and proper place, and there grant him every indulgence necessary for the preservation of his health consistent with the safekeeping of his person; and that the commanding officer in this place afford the necessary assistance of guards for that purpose."*

But this was not the end of the case. On December 27th Batwell presented a second petition that he "be enlarged on parole for the safety of his private affairs and the reestablishment of his health." A certificate from Dr. Robert Henry, surgeon for prisoners at the gaol, testified "that the petitioner labors under a complication of disorders and that clean air, and gentle exercise are absolutely necessary for his recovery."

Congress, accordingly, moved that he be allowed to go to his farm near York Springs upon giving his parole "to hold no correspondence with the enemies of the United States nor to do anything whatever to the prejudice of the American Cause." When this motion received only five affirmative votes, a second one was proposed and executed:

> *"Resolved, That in the opinion of Congress, the Rev. Mr. Batwell should be discharged out of confinement, on his taking an oath of allegiance to the State of Pennsylvania; or, on his refusal, that he should be allowed to go with his family into the city of Philadelphia."*

These two incidents of loyalist actively on the part of well educated and influential citizens, although posing no real threat to security, emphasized the need for strong, decisive action. Other "Duchés" and "Batwells", all too numerous throughout the 13 states, must not be allowed to undermine the national confidence, already weakened by the loss of Philadelphia, the impotence of the army, and the flight of Congress. Samuel Adams, that greatest of all agitators, addressing an early October caucus at the home of General Roberdeau, put this feeling into words:

> *"The eyes of the people of this country are upon us here, and the tone of their feeling is regulated by ours. If we as delegates in Congress give up in despair, and grow desperate, public confidence will be destroyed and American liberty will be no more..."*

The men who listened to Samuel Adams warning them against despondency and stressing the need to "inspire the people with confidence in us, in themselves, and in the cause of their country", fully understood the purport of his words. They knew that "if their rights were to be established and their liberty secured", the council hall must become an extension of the battlefield. They had already proclaimed to the world, as Adams reminded them, their "determination to die free men rather than live slaves." Now that proclamation must be translated into legislation which would unite those free and independent colonies into a free and independent nation.

Such legislation had been under way since 1776, but because of conflicting interests and political differences, Congress had been unable to agree on the specifics of confederation. It was to his unfinished business, the task of completing and adopting the ARTICLES OF CONFEDERATION AND PERPETUAL UNION, that the delegates in York Town now addressed themselves with all the determination and diplomacy at their command. Entrenched at the baize-covered tables in the Court House, these weary warriors, armed with "goose quills, ink and the English language" fought the loneliest and most decisive battle of the war for American Independence.

The Voice of A New Nation

When Martin Breneise rang the Court House bell on those frosty fall mornings of 1777, the men who answered its summons were of divergent backgrounds and convictions. Among the delegates debating the Articles of Confederation were men of great personal fortune, John Hancock of Massachusetts and Charles Carroll of Carrollton, the wealthiest man in America. There were the sons of proud old American families, the Lees of Virginia, Arthur Middleton of South Carolina. There were the wealthy merchants, Robert Morris and Daniel Roberdeau of Pennsylvania, Henry Laurens of South Carolina. There was New York's William Duer, one of the first manufacturers of cotton goods in the country. There were Physicians, men of law and letters, educated at Harvard, William and Mary, Eton, Edinburgh and the Inns of Court. There were others with less formal education and few intellectual or cultural attainments — men of limited means and limited resources. There were firebrand revolutionaries such as John Adams and Samuel Adams (whose poverty was his pride) and staunch conservatives. There were seasoned veterans of the First Continental Congress, Signers of the Declaration of Independence, and newcomers who, like Laurens, Roberdeau, Harnett, Duer, and William Smith of Maryland, had taken their seats only a few months before.

Compounding these personal differences were the differences in the political structure of the states they represented. Prior to the Declaration of Independence, Massachusetts, with its own independent charter, had a governor appointed by the King: the unique charters of Connecticut and

69

Rhode Island had permitted domestic control of executive offices; Pennsylvania, Delaware and Maryland, as proprietary provinces, had been administered by their proprietors, the Penns and the Calverts. The assemblies of the remaining colonies, with no charters of their own, had been more directly dominated by the Crown.

State Constitutions   Immediately upon the abolishment of British rule, each of the thirteen free and independent states hastened to exercise its new-found sovereignty by drafting its own constitution and electing its own executives. But thirteen separate states, acting independently under thirteen separate governments, could not secure "the unalienable rights of life, liberty and the pursuit of happiness" for America as a whole. The same document which proclaimed a people's right to abolish an existing form of government, created the responsibility for establishing a new one, "most likely to effect their Safety and Happiness." Thus it was inherent within the Declaration itself that some form of permanent union be established on American soil.

Richard Henry Lee's original motion for Independence (June 7, 1776) included the additional provision: "That a plan of confederation be prepared and transmitted to the respective colonies for their consideration and approbation." To some delegates it was "putting the cart before the horse" to declare independence before such a plan was in operation. Nevertheless, on June 11th and 12th, Congress did sufficiently agree that a proper confederation was necessary for "internal peace and union" as to appoint a 13 man committee "to prepare and digest the form of confederation."

On July 12th the Articles of Confederation and Perpetual Union, as drafted by John Dickinson of Pennsylvania, were presented to Congress and copies secretly distributed for consideration by individual states.

Now, fifteen months later, in the Court House at York Town, those very articles, rewritten, revised, amended and re-amended were still under fire and time was running out. If European alliances and treaties were to be successfully negotiated, currency stabalized, military disaster averted, and public confidence restored, Congress must have the power to act for a united people. Speed was of the essence.

Beginning with October 2nd, when it was "Resolved that the Articles of Confederation be taken into consideration tomorrow morning at 11 o'Clock", the Journals, as recorded at York Town, carried almost daily entries pertaining to this complex and pressing business. Since the Journals were not the accounts of individuals, but the accepted records of Congress, they reflected the opinions of its members only as expressed in the final votes on motions that were duly accepted or rejected. Thus, a tally of "the yeas and nays required" for a given motion to "Pass in the affirmative" or "in the negative" gave no hint of the controversy and compromise preceding the adoption of the several articles.

The three issues which aroused the most passionate disagreement among the delegates were the manner of voting, the apportionment of expenses and the power of Congress to "settle the claims to the South Seas," which meant the fixing of western boundaries.

Goaded by the urgency of the times, Congress was determined on the earliest possible settlement of these differences. But the Godfrey Lenhart timepiece in the little court room was to tick off many a long hour before "thirteen clocks were made to strike together, a perfection of mechanisms which" as John Adams observed, "no artist had ever before effected."

Clock No. 30
made by
Godfrey Lenhart

The 13 states, like the 13 clocks, were of assorted shapes and sizes, of different design and of different components. Continuing the analogy, even though they might eventually strike together, the deep tones of the "Grand-fathers" must not drown out the tinkling chimes of the smaller mantle clocks or wag-a-walls.

Decisions at York Town would determine not only confederation itself, but the nature of the union to be effected: a national state-or a union of independent states.

Thus the issue of representation pitted the smaller states against the larger. The original motion "in determining questions in the United States in Congress assembled, each State shall have one vote" was hotly contested. On the one hand was the rumor that the larger colonies threatened not to confederate at all unless their weight in Congress was proportionate to their population. On the other hand, it was reported that the smaller states would reject any union which denied them an equal voice in the protection of their rights.

These conflicting interests are aptly illustrated by the opposing stands of the gentlemen from New Jersey and Massachusetts Bay. The Rev. Dr. Witherspoon, supporting the one-vote-proposition, saw himself and his fellow members as representatives of separate Colonies — not as representatives of individuals within those colonies. But because those states or colonies were made up of people, John Adams was equally convinced that it was the people he represented. Therefore, his logic dictated that any system of voting must be in proportion to their numbers.

So the battle lines were drawn and the verbal conflict began. Like the poet's "Men of Indostan", the gentlemen of Congress "disputed loud and long, each in his own opinion, exceeding stiff and strong", although as the verse concludes, and as history has demonstrated, "Each was partly in the right, and all were in the wrong!"

Not only were the states divided, but some of their delegates differed among themselves. John Adams held out against Samuel Adams and Eldridge Gerry. South Carolina's Arthur Middleton opposed Thomas Heyward, Jr. and Henry Laurens. John Penn's vote cancelled that of his fellow North Carolinian, Cornelius Harnett. But, fortunately, by the close of the October 7th session, perhaps out of sheer exhaustion, they reached an agreement. The original motion was reintroduced and passed; the final tally — ten states in the Affirmative, Virginia in the Negative, North

Carolina Divided, Delaware, not represented.

Cornelius Harnett reported to his Governor as follows:

"Congress have once more begun to think of confederation. I could wish to know the sentiments of our General Assembly upon some Capital points. The method of voting by states was yesterday determined. viz, that each State should have one vote, no Colony against it, but Virginia. The grand point of settling the Quota of Taxes each State is to pay comes on this afternoon. Three proposals have been made, one to tax by the Poll, another to assess the value of the Lands, and the other to assess property in general. The latter at present I think most equitable. Should the Confederation be agreed upon, Mr. Penn and myself will embrace the earliest opportunity of transmitting it to your Excellency to be laid before the General Assembly. The Delegates of the Several States are exceedingly anxious to finish this business, many assert that the very Salvation of these States depend upon it; and that none of the European powers will publicly acknowledge them free and independent, until they are confederated."

On the plans submitted for equitable taxation the states were again divided, this time their interpretation of the terms "property" and "people" being the chief cause of disagreement.

Property or Population

Samuel Chase of Maryland contended that it would be inequitable to place a tax on the head of his slave, since a slave is property. Were you to do this, he argued, you would then have to place a tax on the head of a farmer in a northern state, and also place a tax on his cattle, since, in his view Negroes should not be considered members of the state more than cattle. Therefore, he proposed that the tax be fixed in accordance with the number of the inhabitants of each state, but the Negro be excluded from the count.

John Adams countered with the proposal that the number of people should be used as an INDEX only, rather than the actual subjects of taxation. "It makes no difference", he argued, "if you call your people freemen or slaves. Ten laborers, whether you call them freemen or slaves, add as much wealth to the state, and it is the wealth of the state that should be taxed. If slaves were overnight transformed into freemen, or freemen were transformed into slaves, in either event, there would still be the same number of laborers contributing to the wealth of the state." Consequently, he wanted to include both slave and freeman in the final count.

On October 10th Henry Laurens confided his growing impatience to his son: *"The present question is the mode of taxation. Two days have been amused with conning it; some sensible things have been said, and as much nonsense as ever I heard in so short a space. I have not contributed to either. I mean to expose my inabilities this Morning in a very few words because I think very few are necessary, and very few would be made, if we were to Tax one State in which all were equally interested. Candour and genuine honesty ought then to be our guides."*

The debates on this issue might have gone on indefinitely had it not been for the voice of Richard Henry Lee of Virginia. To his motion "that the public expense be apportioned according to the estimated value of land and improvements in each state", he added a strong plea for compromise:

"In so moving I must note that in this great business of forming our first common charter, we must yield a little to each other, and no rigidly insist on having everything correspond to our own partial views. On such basis we would never be able to confederate."

By October 14th when the final vote was taken, the cast of characters in the Court House drama was somewhat altered. Dr. Jonathan Elmer had joined his colleague, Mr. Witherspoon from New Jersey, Dr. Thomas Burke had taken his seat at the North Carolina table, and the gentlemen from Georgia, Dr. Brownson and George Walton, had taken their departure, leaving that state temporarily without representation. With only eleven of the thirteen states voting, the tax problem, one of the thorniest issues of the confederation, was settled by the narrowest margin: 5 in favor, 4 opposed, Pennsylvania and New York, divided.

So the debates continued, Article after Article, Section after Section. Happily, there were some provisions which met with prompt and unanimous acceptance

Article 4 — providing that the free inhabitant of any state may enjoy the same privileges in any other state.

Article 5 — providing for no less than two nor no more than seven delegates from any one state.

Article 6 — prohibiting any state from entering into any separate treaty with any foreign power.

Article 11 — providing for the admission of Canada into the Confederacy.

But other Articles came under the closest scrutiny for exactness of wording and clarity of content. Article Two, for example, was of such fundamental importance that it was read and re-read. There must be no loophole for misinterpretation in the proviso that "Each state retain its

sovereignty, freedom and independence and every power, jurisdiction and right, which is not by this Confederation expressly delegated to the United States, in Congress assembled.''

In the midst of a war for independence, an armed rebellion against the strong central government as represented by the British Crown, no state could risk losing its right of self-government to any individual or legislative body. The King must not be permitted to return in any form or guise.

By this one article John Dickinson's philosophy of a strong central government as expressed in his original draft of the Confederation was clearly and specifically reversed.

It was partly this same fear of vesting too much power in a single body which delayed decision on the question of who should have control of the land to the west of the 13 original colonies. Should it be the states who claimed such land by reason of their royal charters, or, should such land be held as an asset to the new nation as a whole?

Despite the defeat of three successive proposals, there was, eventually, sufficient agreement on a somewhat complicated plan for the settlement of boundary disputes by a panel of especially selected judges, as to be included in the final draft submitted for ratification.

As the Articles approached completion, Congress proceeded with infinite care and caution. Motions were made and challenged, arguments and counter-arguments were advanced, and votes were cast on the insertion. alteration or revision of a single word or phrase. Although tedious and time-consuming, this ''fine-tooth-comb'' process was neither petty nor picayune. These men were determined that if this charter was to be (as it was later described) ''The Constitutional Embodiment of the Declaration of Independence'', it must, in no way, contradict or imperil the principles set forth in that document. Unless the Articles were comprehensible and acceptable to the Congress as a whole, they would not stand a chance of being ratified by the individual states. Every sentence, therefore, must be measured, every word must be weighed, every syllable counted.

As the brilliance of October faded into the bleakness of November, there came the long awaited confirmation of the great American victory at Saratoga. For weeks there had been persistent rumors of Burgoyne's defeat, but no official word from General Gates. Finally, on the last day of October, a tardy but impenitent Colonel Wilkinson arrived with dispatches from his commanding officer. The previous reports, almost too good to be

true, the rumors which had "lifted them to the Stars", were fully and gloriously verified. "Gentleman Johnny" Burgoyne and his whole army had laid down their arms in total surrender to a former British regular, General Horatio Gates.

The wave of rejoicing about to sweep the country was not to be wasted. As the classical scholars in Congress remembered their Latin, "Carpe Diem", the rest recalled the old adage to "Make hay while the sun shines!" Bu every political instinct, they recognized the upswing of public morale as the perfect opportunity for presenting the Articles of Confederation to the people. As the November days grew shorter, the candles in the Court House were lighted earlier and burned later. The quill pens scratched with increasing speed, crossing out a word here, changing a phrase there, until, finally, on November 15th the task was finished.

Resignation of Hancock

But during that last frenzied fortnight, some notable changes had taken place. On October 29th John Hancock, who had served as President of Congress for two years and five months, resigned, and on November first, Henry Laurens of South Carolina was unanimously elected to that office. As Hancock rose from the Justice Bench for the last time to address his colleagues, he must have realized the enormity of their continuing responsibilities. Pleading impaired health and the absolute necessity for some relaxation after so long a term of service, he concluded his formal farewell with these words:

> *"I cannot take my departure, gentlemen, without expressing my thanks for the civility and politeness I have experienced from you. It is impossible to mention this without a heartfelt pleasure.*
>
> *If, in the course of so long a period as I have had the honor to fill this chair, any expressions may have dropped from me that may have given the least offence to any member, as it was not intentional, so I hope his candor will pass it over.*
>
> *May every happiness, gentlemen, attend you, both as members of this house and as individuals; and I pray heaven, that unanimity and preserverance may go hand in hand in this house; and that everything which may tend to distract or divide your councils be forever banished."*

But President Hancock's prayer for unaminity was not immediately granted. As his blanket apology for unintended offenses would indicate, he was not the most popular of men, especially among the New England delegates, and it required two separate motions on the floor before it was agreed by a 5 to 4 vote that he receive the official thanks of Congress for

"the unremitted attention and steady impartiality which he has manifested in discharge of the various duties of his office."

Samuel Adams, writing to James Warren of the Massachusetts legislature, remained unconvinced of the propriety of the action:

> *"We have had two Presidents before (Peyton Randolph and Henry Middleton) neither of whom made a parting Speech or received The Thanks of Congress."*

Nevertheless, Hancock departed, not only with thanks, but also with an impressive retinue. William Ellery of Rhode Island, on his way to York in the company of Francis Dana of Massachusetts, described their meeting with the retiring president near Fishkill, New York:

> *"On our way to the Fishkill Ferry we met President Hancock in a sulkey, escorted by one of his Secretaries and two or three other gentlemen, and one light horse-man (returning from Congress at Yorktown). The escort surprised us as it seemed inadequate to the purpose either of defense or parade. But our surprise was not of long circumstances; for we had not rode far before we met six or eight Light horse-men on the canter, and just as we reached the Ferry, a boat arrived with many more — all making up the escort of President Hancock. Who would not be a great man? I verily believe that the President as he passed through the Country thus escorted, feels a more triumphant satisfaction than the Colonel of the Queen's Regiment of Light Dragoons attended by his whole army and escort of a thousand Militia."*

Since these two delegates were making the four hundred fifty mile journey on horseback, unattended except for a single man-servant, riding behind them, the somewhat caustic tone of the description is understandable.

But Hancock was not the only Massachusetts member to leave for home. On the 8th of November, with far less fanfare, Samuel Adams, waiting only for the adoption of the most controversial Articles of Confederation, took his departure; and, a few days later, John Adams, who had begun to fear he would "scarcely know his own children", were he to be away much longer, also set off for Boston. As he mounted his "little pony" in front of General Roberdeau's house on George Street, and rode northward through the Square, Adams could not possibly have foreseen that his next visit to the familiar little Court House would be as the second President of the United States.

The leadership of these two veterans of the First Continental

Congress, so different in personality and background, but so similar in their dedication to the Cause, would be sorely missed by the new President of Congress. However, regardless of who came or went, regardless of new problems and increasing pressures, the completion of the Confederation must retain its priority.

November 15, 1977 A Date to Remember

And so it followed on November 15, 1777 that Congress finally adopted the

ARTICLES OF CONFEDERATION AND PERPETUAL UNION

BETWEEN THE STATES OF

NEW HAMPSHIRE,	*PENNSYLVANIA,*
MASSACHUSETTS BAY,	*DELAWARE,*
RHODE ISLAND AND PROVIDENCE	*MARYLAND,*
PLANTATIONS,	*VIRGINIA,*
CONNECTICUT,	*NORTH CAROLINA,*
NEW YORK,	*SOUTH CAROLINA,*
NEW JERSEY,	*GEORGIA.*

The bulky manuscript was carefully copied by Charles Thomson and dispatched to Lancaster where 300 copies were printed and prepared for distribution by Francis Bailey of that place.

Congress was the first to admit that the finished Articles were far from perfect. Although rejecting the dire prophecy of John Adams "that before ten years, this confederation, like a rope of sand, will be found inadequate to the purpose and its dissolution will take place", they were well aware of its inherent weakness. They knew that many of the same issues which had divided their own members would, in turn, divide the state legislatures.

Anticipating the opposition of Dr. Thomas Burke, recently returned to the North Carolina Assembly, Cornelius Harnett reported to him as follows:

> *"The child Congress has been big with, these two years past, is at last brought forth. I fear it will by several Legislatures be thought a little deformed. You will think it a Monster."*

Acutely conscious of these imperfections or "deformities", Congress drafted a circular letter to accompany the Articles, acknowledging them to be the product of compromise and conciliation and pleading for the liberality of judgment requiring to make individual sacrifices for the common good: The letter pointed out —

> *"To form a permanent union, accommodated to the opinion and wishes of*

the delegates of so many states, differing in habits, produce, commerce, and internal police, was found to be a work which nothing but time and reflection, conspiring with a disposition to conciliate, could mature and accomplish.

Hardly is it to be expected that any plan, in the variety of provisions essential to our union, should exactly correspond with the maxims and political views of every particular State. Let it be remarked, that after the most careful enquiry and the fullest information, this is proposed as the best which could be adapted to the circumstance of all; and as that alone which affords any tolerable prospect of a general ratification.''

''The best which could be adapted to the circumstances of all.''

But in spite of their awareness of the inflammatory nature of the individual articles, Congress was unshaken on the validity and immediate necessity of confederation. The letter, which was in itself a minor masterpiece, continued with the statement:

''More than any other consideration, it will confound our foreign enemies, defeat the flagitious practices of the disaffected, strengthen and confirm our friends, support our public credit, restore and value of our money, enable us to maintain our fleets and armies, and add weight and respect to our councils at home, and to our treaties abroad.''

To the townspeople going about their business on Saturday, November 15th, 1777, the Court House appeared the same as usual. The farmers crowding the open market sheds, the housewives bargaining for plump chickens or succulent geese, the small children clinging to their mothers' skirts or racing madly around the Square did not pause to give it a second glance. A clean-conscious hausfrau might have noted that the windows needed washing or that the steps could do with a good scrubbing, but there were no visible signs that the building had been touched by greatness.

Court House to Capitol

None the less, the titanic achievment within that early citadel of law and justice would forever leave its mark. In only forty five days the delegates to Congress there assembled reconciled the differences which had so long divided them. They had completed and adopted ''a plan of Confederacy for securing freedom, sovereignty and independence'', thereby creating the first constitutional government of the New World. These men were, in truth, the ''forefathers who brought forth upon this continent a new nation.'' It was by this action and on this date that the first Court

House of York County became, in fact and by law, the First Capitol of the United States of America.

Commemorative stamp in recognition of the adoption of The Articles of Confederation in York Town.

Shouts of Victory
Prayers of Thanksgiving

The fifty three year old Henry Laurens, who moved from the South Carolina table to "a good seat near a warm fire", on the President's bench, November 1, 1777, was a wealthy planter-merchant of French Huguenot ancestry. A man of strong administrative ability, proven patriotism, and ready wit, he was described by Daniel Roberdeau, at the time of his election, as "a worthy, sensible, indefatigable Gentleman." After only a month's acquaintenance, John Adams had been liberal in his praise: "They have sent us a new delegate whom I greatly admire, Mr. Laurens, their Lieutenant Governor, a gentleman of great fortune, great abilities, modesty and integrity, and great experience, too. If all the states send us such men, it would be a pleasure to be here."

The new President, in his turn, had had four months in which to assess Congress and their often ponderous procedures. He had sat through many a session dealing with army affairs which, in many cases, had better been left to the military. But Congress, ever mindful of the incipient threat of a standing army to "the Liberties of a People," was determined to maintain the supremacy of civil government. Their concerns were endless: the conferring of commissions, promotions within the ranks, the deployment of troops, pay, equipment, supplies, prisoners of war, court martials, recruitment, desertion, even such minutiae as the granting of individual leaves and the number of vests issued to officers, — "two for winter, one for summer". No military or civil matters were too large or too small to claim their attention. In the midst of debating the Articles of Confederation and

Henry Laurens, 1724-1792, President of Continental Congress

82

negotiating with foreign powers, a resolution was passed for the importing of 20,000 Bibles from Holland and Scotland, and a committee was appointed "to collect and digest the late useful discoveries for making molasses and spirits from the juice of cornstalks."

Small wonder Charles Carroll of Carrollton should have written: "The Congress do worse than ever; we murder time and chat away in idle, impertinent talk!"

But there were no petty distractions on Laurens' first day in office. Such was the overwhelming rejoicing over the triumph at Saratoga that only one item of business was transacted — the unanimous approval of a recommendation to set apart a day of thanksgiving for this signal victory. As this national proclamation, drafted by Richard Henry Lee, Samuel Adams, and Daniel Roberdeau, was read before the House, the members listened with respect and reverence:

The First National Thanksgiving Proclamation

> *"Forasmuch as it is the indispensable duty of all men to adore the superintending providence of Almighty God; to acknowledge with gratitude their obligation to him for benefits received and to implore such farther blessings as they stand in need of; and it having pleased him in his abundant mercy not only to continue to us the innumerable bounties of his common providence, but also to smile upon us in the prosecution of a just and necessary war, for the defence and establishment of our unalienable rights and liberties; particularly in that he hath been pleased in so great a measure to prosper the means used for the support of our troops and to crown our arms with most signal success; it is therefore recommended to the legislative or executive powers of these United States, to set apart Thursday, the eighteenth day of December next, for solemn thanksgiving and praise; that with one heart and one voice the good people may express the grateful feelings of their hearts, and consecrate themselves to the service of their devine benefactor . . . .*
> *And it is further recommended, that servile labor, and such recreation as, though at other times innocent, may be unbecoming the purpose of this appointment, to be omitted on so solemn an occasion."*

Within a week the document was in the hands of the printer. The lack of printing facilities in York, a serious inconvenience to Congress, had been remedied by action of October 17th, when the Hall and Sellers Press, removed from Philadelphia to Lancaster for safekeeping, was ordered to York. By this time, it had arrived and was installed in the residence of Major John Clark at the South West Corner of Market and Beaver Streets. It was

Printed in York Town

on this historic press, once the property of Benjamin Franklin that the National Thanksgiving Proclamation, the first ever issued in the United States, was printed and made ready for distribution to the governors of the thirteen states.

And on this same press, by order of the Committee of Intelligence, were printed the terms of surrender known as THE ARTICLES OF CONVENTION between Lieutenant General Burgoyne and Major General Gates, as signed at Saratoga, October 16, 1777 and delivered two weeks later to Congress at York Town.

There was every reason for jubilation and thanksgiving for Burgoyne's capitulation. Saratoga had cost the enemy Ticonderoga and Crown Point, seven generals, three hundred or more assorted officers, five thousand men at arms and a full complement of supplies and material. The victory was later judged to be the turning point of the war, Saratoga, "the most decisive battle ever fought on American soil." It bolstered American morale, weakened British confidence on the home front to the point of considering overtures for peace, and strengthened French resolve to continue her support and openly aid the United States.

But as Congress studied the shockingly generous terms of surrender, terms dictated by Burgoyne and hastily accepted by Gates under threat of Clinton's rapid advance toward Albany, it became obvious that the "Convention" might turn triumph into disaster. If, as the treaty permitted, Burgoyne's whole army were to sail out of Boston back to England, it would be like the old rhyme: "He who fights and gets away, lives to fight another day!" Even if Burgoyne kept his word that his men should not again serve in North America during the war, their return would release an equal number of men on active duty as replacements. This could not be allowed. Burgoyne must not have the opportunity to laugh up his silken sleeve at the colonials who had won a battle but lost the peace. A second battle must be fought to defend the victory achieved at Saratoga. And this battle, a battle of wits, was fought on the floor of the York County Court House.

It was Washington himself who sounded the first call for diplomatic action in a warning addressed to Richard Henry Lee.

> *"I am nevertheless convinced, that this event (the surrender of Burgoyne) will not equal our expectations; and that, without great precausion, and very delicate management, we shall have all these men — if not the officers — opposed to us in the spring. Without the necessary precautions,*

"The harder the conflict, the more glorious the triumph."
Thomas Paine

(as I have just observed) I think this will happen; and unless great delicacy is used in the precautions, a plea will be given them, and they will justify, a breach of the Covenant on their part — do they not declare (many of them) that no faith is to be held with the Rebels?"

Congress was, indeed, on dangerous ground. The convention had already been signed. To repudiate any of its terms would be an affront to General Gates — the Man of the Hour — and might also tarnish America's reputation among the very European nations whose confidence they were hoping to win. But they could and did take the precautions Washington advised. On November 8, 1777 the following resolution was adopted: *On Dangerous Ground*

"That Major General Heath (in command at Boston) be directed forthwith to cause to be taken down the name and rank of every commissioned officer, and the name, former place of abode, occupation, size, age, and description of every non-commissioned officer and private soldier, and all other persons comprehended in the convention made between Lieutenant General Burgoyne and Major General Gates on the 16 day of October, 1777, and transmit an authentic copy thereof to the Board of War, in order that if any officer, soldier, or other person, as above mentioned, of the said army, shall hereafter be found in arms against these states in North America during the present contest, he may be convicted of the offence, and suffer the punishment in such case inflicted by the law of nations.

That Major General Heath be directed to take the parole in writing of the officers according to the convention, and transmit authenticated copies of such paroles to the Board of War."

Not only did Burgoyne refuse to comply with these demands, which implied some doubt of his honorable intentions, but he launched an attack of his own, charging that the "Public Faith" had already been broken by Heath's failure to provide suitable quarters for his officers, according to rank, as guaranteed by Article VII of the convention.

His complaints to Gates, that six or seven officers were crowded into a room about 10 feet square and that he himself was forced to pay an exorbitant sum for a house, were as absurd as they were infuriating. "Absurd" — because Boston and its environs, with an influx of 7,000 outsiders, were so over-crowded that any lodgings were virtually impossible at any price; "Infuriating" — because they came from the commander of Indians and mercenaries who, by public proclamation, had threatened the countryside with "devastation, famine and every concommitant horror!"

To the men of Congress, not too conveniently lodged themselves, and currently investigating Howe's "shocking inhumanity" to American prisoners in Philadelphia, reportedly dying of starvation, Burgoyne's charges were fighting words.

On December 18, the day set apart for "thanksgiving, prayers and repentance", Congress attended service in the Reformed Church where they heard a sermon delivered in English by Pastor Neisser of the Moravian congregation. But by three o'clock in the afternoon they were, figuratively, manning their battle stations at the Court House.

If Great Britain chose to press Burgoyne's accusation that "The Public Faith is broke", the United States could be seriously discredited and the whole convention declared invalid. Congress must defend its own position that any breach of faith which had occurred had been the doing of Burgoyne himself, and there was plenty of ammunition.

Article VI, which protected Officers' baggage from search and molestation on Burgoyne's honour that no public stores were secreted therein, had been openly and brazenly violated. The regimental colors had vanished. The number of muskets was less than the number of prisoners and the number of bayonets less than the number of muskets, all of which were unfit for service. Officers had kept their cartouche boxes, their scabbards and belts. The military chest and medicines were not accounted for. On and on went the discrepancies reported by the committee in charge of receiving captured ordnance and stores.

Congress had already rejected General Howe's request to change the port of embarkation from Boston to some other port under British control, and had discovered that his ships' stores were insufficient for a voyage across the Atlantic. President Laurens, Lafayette, Washington and other leaders shared the suspicion of a treacherous plot to land the evacuated armies at some occupied American port where they could be reorganized for active duty.

This was the state of affairs when Congress met on that cold Thanksgiving afternoon to consider a counter-offensive to the charges of Burgoyne as delivered in a letter from General Gates. A committee of five was appointed to draw up the battle plan: John Witherspoon of New Jersey, Francis Dana of Massachusetts, Francis Lightfoot Lee of Virginia, William Duer of New York and the new delegate from Pennsylvania, Jonathan Bayard Smith, who had taken his seat that very day. As chairman, Dr.

Witherspoon, educated as a Presbyterian Divine at Edinburgh and President of the College of New Jersey (renamed Princeton in 1894) displayed all the wit and wile of a born strategist in manoeuvring to keep Burgoyne and his army in American hands.

Equally determined to suspend the convention was President Henry Laurens. In addition to struggling with the unaccustomed rigors of a severe northern winter, a weakened and rapidly decreasing Congress (reduced to 19 members) Laurens had the added burden of being the sole representative of his home state. He was also fighting a losing battle with an attack of gout. The severity of this physical disability is described in a letter resigning the presidency, dated "12, Decem, 1777."

> *"Your President has been confined to his Chamber and in Bed for three days and Nights past during which time he has not had three hours sleep, the Malady under which he labours has made such a progress as to convince him by reflecting upon former attacks that he will not be able to move out of the House nor to attend his duty in Congress for some Weeks to come. When he accepted the Honour which you were pleased to confer on him it was with a single Eye to your service in the most comprehensive meaning. Now he finds himself incapable of performing his duty he is anxious to Resign that Honour which he accepted only in obedience to your Vote..."*

A reluctant Resignation

In spite of his expressed fears that public business would be impeded and some branches would run into confusion, his resignation was not accepted, and Henry Laurens struggled on. As he had anticipated, his condition worsened. By the end of this month, as indicated in a letter to his close friend, John Lewis Gervais, he was in a pitiable state:

30th, Decem. 1777

> *"My Dear Friend,*
>
> *I am now sitting both feet and Legs bound up in a Blanket in the room where Congress meets, between the adjournment at 1/2p: one oClock and meeting hour at three, and where a scrap of some what will be sent for my repast to serve till tomorrow's breakfast. Perhaps two, it may be three, hours after dark, I may be permitted to hobble on my Crutches over Ice and frozen snow, or to be carried to such a homely home as I have, where I must sit in Bed one or two or three hours longer at the writing Table, pass the remainder of a tedious night in pain and some anxiety."*

The day after Christmas, according to this same letter, Laurens, in spite of his suffering, permitted himself to be carried to the Court House in order that the business which he had "set or caused to be set in motion" — the business of the Saratoga Convention — might be "treated with the greatest Solemnity in a full Representation."

Without once specifying the exact nature of "the business which had been the subject of his meditation and contemplation through several Sleepless nights and Days", Laurens clearly described to his trusted friend, the importance of the fateful action Congress was about to take in accepting the Committee's recommendations for dealing with Burgoyne's perfidious charges and delaying, if not entirely preventing, the embarkation of his troops.

The Committee had prepared a thorough and devastating report. After a lengthy and detailed summation of British violation of terms and a forceful rebuttal of Burgoyne's charges, branded as an excuse to disengage himself from his obligations to the United States, Congress solemnly resolved to ratify the convention and "cause the prisoners surrendered by virtue of it to be released" . . . . . . BUT

Master of Strategy   Here Witherspoon had master-minded an extra, conditional resolution:

> *"Resolved, therefore, That the embarkation of Lieutenant-General Burgoyne, and the troops under his command, be suspended until a distinct and explicit ratification of the convention of Saratoga shall be properly notified by the Court of Great Britain to Congress."*

This was a ploy that was worthy of a Portia. Indeed, the wily Witherspoon might well have chortled: "Now, by King George, I have thee on the hip!" Compliance with this demand to treat with Congress would be a technical recognition of the United States as an independent nation — a condition the Crown could not possibly accept. But refusal would automatically free this government to detain Burgoyne and his army on American soil.

Although Laurens exulted in the British dilemma, he was well aware of possible international repercussions. In his lengthy letter to Gervais, he was speaking for every member of Congress when he alluded to his own signature on this document as "a signature which will be put before the Tribunal of the Whole Civilized World."

Would American Honour be tainted by the imposition of this additional condition to a treaty already signed, or would it be vindicated by indisputable evidence of British treachery?

More than a century and a half later, American suspicions of a scheme to abort the return voyage to England and dispatch the captured prisoners to active duty were fully confirmed by Sir Henry Clinton's Secret Service papers released to scholars for the first time. But at the time the pain-racked President of Congress was agonizing over the problem, he could only say: "Whether it be determined by the World to be good or bad, the Act is great, and great good or evil will follow as its consequences."

"The Great Act", opposed by some members, described by Laurens as "timerous dunces", was not adopted in its final form until January 8, 1778. In March Burgoyne, on a plea of ill health, received permission to return to England where he was the object of severe criticism by the press and parliament. When the snows at Valley Forge had melted and Washington's army was once more on the move, the convention troops which might have borne arms against him were prisoners of war and remained so until the end of the Revolution.

Throughout all the long weeks of deliberation over the convention settlement, there had been no overt criticism of Gates, "The Hero of Saratoga." He had won his victory by the sword. Congress confirmed it by the pen. It was at the Court House in York Town that the United States was created by the Articles of Confederation, and it was in the Court House at York Town that the new nation first refused to negotiate with the enemy except on the basis of communication between one sovereign state and another. Any comparison between the York County Court House and Westminster Hall would be ludicrous, but they had one thing in common. Each was the seat of a national government — one old and established — the other, new and uncertain, engaged in a struggle for survival. The suspension of the Saratoga Convention advanced that struggle one step closer to a triumphant conclusion.

Murmurs of Dissent

Whispers of Conspiracy

8

As December of 1777 blew itself to a blustery close, the members of Congress wrapped the heavy, long table-coverings more closely around their shivering shanks, and heated more and more bricks on the Court House stove for their inadequate foot-warmers. President Laurens was not the only victim of gout. Cornelius Harnett suffered from the same ailment, and many of the others, whose average age was forty six, were subject to various disabilities. The foot-warners, thrust under the tables, provided an extra measure of comfort to the sick and the well as they listened to Secretary Thomson read a reproachful letter from the Commander-in-Chief the day after Christmas.

> *"I can assure these Gentlemen that it is a much easier and less distressing thing to draw remonstrances in a comfortable room by a good fire side than to occupy a cold, bleak hill and sleep under frost and snow without Cloaths or Blankets; however, although they seem to have little feeling for the naked, and distressed Soldier, I feel superabundantly for them, and from my soul pity those miseries which it is neither in my power to relieve or prevent . . . and it adds not a little to my other difficulties, and distress, to find that much more is expected of me than is possible to perform and that upon the ground of safety and policy, I am obliged to conceal the true State of the Army from Public view and thereby expose myself to detraction and Calumny."*

Actually Congress was not as insensitive to the situation at Valley Forge as Washington's letter would indicate. The General's pique stemmed from a Resolution of December 10, requesting that he "should endeavor, as much as possible, to subsist his army upon such parts of the country as are in its vicinity", and urging that he use the full weight of the powers granted him by Congress to confiscate or destroy "all provisions, stores, forage, waggons and teams" which might otherwise be used by the enemy.

But the area of Valley Forge had been virtually stripped clean in September. The State Assembly was slow to comply with congressional orders for grain and foodstuffs. Shipments of clothing, blankets, meat and flour from other states failed to reach their destination either by reason of impassable roads or sheer bungling.

"The Winter of Discontent" The unusual bitterness of Washington's reaction to this mild criticism was but one of many indications that "The Year of the Hangman" was about to be replaced by "The Winter of Discontent." And that discontent was as deep-seated as it was wide-spread.

The ill-informed Public was discontented and disillusioned by military losses and economic hardships which they could not understand, but which they blamed jointly on the Army and Congress.

The tatterdemalions at Valley Forge, discontented with their unhappy lot, were either deserting or cursing a government whose largesse had, so far, consisted of "half a gill of rice and a tablespoon full of vinegar" issued on the December 18th Thanksgiving Day.

Washington and his staff were discontented with the incompetency (or deliberate neglect) of the Board of War, Commissary and Quarter-master Departments which left wagon loads of clothing and provisions standing at supply depots or abandoned in the woods.

The Board of War was discontented with Washington's leadership, his failure to attack Howe and the apparent lack of organization and discipline within the army.

President Laurens was discontented and alarmed by the general apathy and by the decline of Congress in both numbers and calibre. By the end of January: "The House has been reduced to 9 States represented in Units...We have sometimes been stagnant for want of numbers, and oftener running whole days into weeks of unmatured conversations from a want of able Members." He implored his own state to "Fill your delegacy in Congress with able man, I say — no frolickers, no jolly fellows!" What Congress needed was not, "more hands" but "more heads", heads filled with the cool wisdom and unbiased judgment demanded by the times. For once, he agreed with Secretary Thomson (with whom he had been known to differ) that this Congress was "a body of weak men with selfish motives". As Gouverneur Morris expressed it: "Continental money and Congress have both deteriorated."

Charles Thomson
1729-1824 only secretary of
Continental Congress
1774-1789 "The Sam
Adams of Philadelphia"
John Adams

This highly charged atmosphere of mistrust and suspicion could very well erupt into a violent explosion were it to be sparked by conspiracy; and such a conspiracy was well under way in the form of what History refers to as THE CONWAY CABAL.

Whether this so-called "Cabal" was an actual organized plot to replace a defeated Washington with a victorious Gates, or merely a conflict between the pro-Washington and anti-Washington factions of Congress is still open to debate. But the name itself has helped preserve the concept of conspiracy.

The very origin of the word CABAL, derived from the Hebrew "Qabbalah" — the mystic interpretation of the scriptures — has overtones of secrecy, of knowledge shared only by a chosen few. "Conway Cabal" makes it easy to say and easy to remember, even by those who do not know who Conway was or what "Cabal" means. "What's in a name?" True — "a rose by any other name would smell as sweet"...but..."The Wilkinson Indiscretion", "The Gates Plan", "The Mifflin Intrigue"...any of these would carry a less sinister aroma. And yet all of these men were as deeply involved in the cabal as the luckless Irishman whose name it bears.

General Thomas Conway, a professional soldier, Irish by birth — French by training and experience, had come to America in the spring of 1777 with the endorsement of Silas Deane, Commissioner to France, and the promise of being made Brigadier General. He received his commission on May 13th of that year.

This circumstance was, in itself, displeasing to Washington. It was a constant irritation to him, an affront to his command, and an embarrassment to Congress to be forced to honor Silas Deane's often grandiose promises by promoting foreign officers over the heads of equally competent or more deserving Continentals. In fact, Washington was both resentful and suspicious of the influx of foreign volunteers, most of whom, with the exception of his loved and trusted Lafayette, he branded as "adventurers", "Men of great ambition who would sacrifice anything for their own glory", or "mere spies" reporting regularly to the courts that sent them.

Writing on this subject at a later date, Washington elaborated:

> *"In the first instance they tell you they wish for nothing more than the honor of serving in so glorious a cause as volunteers, the next day solicit rank without pay, the day following want money advanced to them, and in the course of a week want further promotion."*

Conway pretty well followed this pattern. Convinced of his own worth and the value of his previous experience, he aspired to a higher rank that would raise his standing when he returned to France.

On first contact with Conway at Morristown, Washington was favorably impressed, calling him "a man of candor" and recommending him to President Laurens. But as the acquaintance ripened, he reversed his judgment; and in October when he learned that Conway had threatened to resign unless he was appointed a major-general, Washington hastily and vigorously opposed his promotion. It was unthinkable that such a braggart should be advanced over 23 older and more deserving brigadiers. Accordingly, Washington advised Richard Henry Lee in York Town:

> *"General Conway's merit...as an officer and his importance in this army exists more in his own imagination than in reality, for it is a maxim with*

him to leave no service of his own untold, nor to want anything which is to be obtained by importunity.''

But Conway had his admirers who, oddly or aptly enough, were antagonistic to Washington and most favorably disposed to Gates. Among them were Quartermaster-General Thomas Mifflin and Dr. Benjamin Rush who championed Conway's cause in a letter to John Adams: ''For God's sake do not suffer him to resign! He is the idol of the whole army!''

Although Rush's appraisal was exaggerated, Conway's conduct at Germantown had won him a fair share of approval from many of his fellow officers but not from the Commander-in-Chief. To Washington he remained ''An incendiary'' . . . ''a man of much intrigue and little judgment.''

''Idol'' or ''Incendiary''

Conway was well aware of this low esteem, but he was even more aware of the increasing disapproval of Washington and the growing popularity of Gates. Why not hitch his wagon to a Rising Star?

With every report from Saratoga the contrast between Gates and Washington grew more pronounced. In York Town the Court House became a forum of unofficial but heated discussions of what Washington did or did not do and what action he should or should not have taken. Henry Laurens described these arm-chair strategists in a letter to his son, Colonel John Laurens, serving as an Aide to Washington:

> *''I am writing in Congress and in the midst of much talk (not regular Congress). 'Buz!' says one: 'I would if I had been Commr. of that army with such powers have procured all the necessaries which are said to be wanted without such whining complaints.'*
>
> *'I would,' says 2d., 'have prevented the amazing desertions which have happened. It only wants proper attention at fountain head.' 3d.: 'It is very easy to prevent intercourse between the army and the enemy and as easy to gain intelligence; but we never mind who comes in and who goes out of our camp.' 'In short,' 4th., 'our army is under no regulation nor discipline,' &c. &c., &c.''*
>
> *''You know I abhor tell tales, but these sounds hurt me exceedingly. I know the effects of loose tongues: I know the cruelty of tongues speaking the fullness of designing hearts . . . .''*

And here, because Laurens knew and understood his son's respect and love for their General, he confided something of his own doubts and fears:

> *''Nevertheless, I am afraid there may be some ground for some of these remarks. A good heart may be too diffident, too apprehensive of doing*

right, righteous, proper acts, lest such should be interpreted arbitrary. But good God, shall we (save) five hundred and destroy five millions? The subject is too delicate to dwell upon."

But if Washington erred on the side of Leniency and "modesty in assuming authority", Gates could not be so accused. His only leniency had been that shown Burgoyne in failing to demand unconditional surrender. And he displayed no undue modesty in accepting credit for the victory made possible to a large extent by Morgan's relentless riflemen and the engineering genius of the Polish volunteer, Thaddeus Kosciusko.

While Washington's errors were being catalogued by Congress, Gates made a few of his own. His first mistake was to violate military procedure by dispatching the news of The Saratoga Triumph to Congress instead of reporting it directly to his Commander, a slight for which he was rebuked in Washington's letter of congratulation.

An Indiscreet Messenger

His second mistake was in his choice of a messenger. Twenty year old Colonel James Wilkinson, entrusted with these most important papers stopped at Reading, Pennsylvania where he spent three days "dallying" with the young lady he later married, and visiting with General Thomas Mifflin who, because of differences with Washington, had recently resigned his post as Quartermaster General. It was as Mifflin's guest, in the presence of Major William McWilliams, an Aide to General (Lord) Stirling, that the reckless young man revealed an excerpt from a letter written by the ambitious Conway designed to flatter Gates at the expense of Washington.

With no premonition of the serious consequences of his impulsive (if not calculated) action, Wilkinson proceeded to York where Congress was so jubilant over his glorious news, that his regrettable delay occasioned only the jocular suggestion that a horsewhip or a pair of spurs might be a more appropriate reward for his services than the promotion recommended by General Gates.

But Wilkinson's disclosure was no joking matter. Major McWilliams saw fit to pass it on to Lord Stirling, also in Reading, recuperating from wounds sustained at Brandywine. Stirling immediately send the offensive paragraph to Washington at White Marsh with the explanation:

"The enclosed was communicated by Colonel Wilkinson to Major McWilliams; such duplicity of conduct I shall always think it my duty to detect."

Washington, who up to this time (November 8th) had no idea that the arrogant Conway was in contact with Gates, gave himself the satisfaction of letting Conway know he was aware of his double dealing. The next day he addressed the following curt note to the offender:

> *"Sir: A letter which I received last night contained the following paragraph:*
>
> *In a letter from General Conway to General Gates, he says: 'Heaven has been determined to save your country, or a weak General and bad counsellors would have ruined it.'*
>
> *I am, Sire, Yr. Hble Servt."*

Conway, taken off guard, immediately wrote what was at once a denial and an apology, protesting that in his opinion Washington was "a brave man, an honest man, a patriot and a man of great sense"; and further avowing that the disgraceful phrase "weak general" had never escaped his pen. He also stated his willingness to submit his original letter to Gates as proof of his innocence. His next move was to tender his resignation, which he rightly assumed Congress would not accept, and then hurried to Reading to consult with General Mifflin. Mifflin's reaction was to alert General Gates at once.

> *"An Extract from General Conway's Letter to you has been procured and sent to Head Quarters. — The Extract was a Collection of just Sentiments yet such as should have not been entrusted to any of your Family —....*
> *My dear General, take care of your Generosity & frank Disposition — they cannot injure yourself but they may injure some of your best Friends."*

Mifflin's warning threw Gates into a state of confusion. Not realizing that Washington had seen only one excerpt from a single letter, and not waiting to check the source of his information, he made another costly mistake. He wrote to Washington intimating that someone had "stealingly copied" from his letters and enlisting his aid in apprehending the spy. He then compounded his error in judgment by adding that since he could not be sure whether the information had been leaked by an officer or by a delegate he had sent a copy of his accusation to Congress.

This communique made Washington take another look at the whole affair. What was going on? He had known of only one letter. Gates spoke of more than one. He had been dealing with the disloyalty of a single officer. Gates was hinting at the possible involvement of other officers and members of Congress. Washington's original annoyance with Conway turned to a more wide-spread suspicion and rage.

He lost no time in setting Gates straight on the Wilkinson-Stirling source of his knowledge. He also sent a copy of this letter to Congress:

"lest any member of that honorable body should harbor an unfavorable suspicion of my having practiced some indirect means to come at the contents of the confidential letters between you and Conway."

The Board of War

All of this complicated correspondence might be dismissed as a staff squabble or a bit of unbecoming back-biting, were it not for the important and highly relevant measures which Congress was taking during this period. In mid-October Congress had confirmed an earlier decision to expedite committee affairs by reorganizing the Board of War to include persons not members of Congress.

Since Congress had specifically resolved that all military and other officers be required to observe the directions of the Board of War, the appointment of these members was of the gravest importance. Could the selection of Gates and Mifflin for these key posts be attributed to coincidence or conniving?

Mifflin was not only appointed to the Board of War, but was also reassigned, against the express wishes of Washington, to the duties of Quarter Master from which "for reasons of ill-health", he had just resigned. The appointment of Gates as the new President of the Board of War on November 27th was more easily explained as a rightful honor due a national hero.

As a reward for his services in the army and for bringing the Saratoga dispatches to Congress the loose-tongued Wilkinson, recommended by Gates as "a gallant officer and a promising military genius," was made brigadier general. And a month later Conway received the promotion which Washington had so vehemently opposed. "The incendiary" was now inspector general of the army with the rank of major general.

Enemies in High Places

Although Washington's enemies were now in high places, his head was unbowed. When, in January, Conway visited Valley Forge in his capacity as Inspector-General, and complained of his chilly reception, Washington forwarded the correspondence to President Laurens with a notation of his own:

"If General Conway means by cool reception . . . that I did not receive him in the language of a warm and cordial friend, I readily confess the charge. I did not, nor shall I ever, till I am capable of the arts of dissimulation. These I despise and my feelings will not permit me to make professions of friendship to the man I deem my enemy and whose system of conduct forbids it. At the same time, Truth authorizes me to say that he was received and

treated with proper respect to his official character and that he has had no cause to justify the assertion that he could not expect any support for fulfilling the duties of his appointment.''

Laurens was probably better informed than any other member of Congress on the complexities of Washington's situation because of the close communication with his son who was an ardent supporter of his Chief and a personal friend of Lafayette. Colonel John Laurens had no doubt that there were ''baneful influences'' at work and did not mince words when he wrote to his father about the Conway letter which, by January, had become common knowledge.

"Conway has weight with a certain party formed against the present Commander-in-Chief, at the head of which is General Mifflin.''

His father, considerably upset with Congress for their disregard of Washington's wishes, was inclined to agree, although he couched his reply in more guarded language:

"I am not quite sure of the fact'', he wrote, ''but I believe you have hit the pivot upon which the late mischiefs have turned. In order, however, to justify this idea, we must include characters of whom your friend (Washington) entertains the most favorable sentiments. These taken together form a club whose demands upon the treasury and the war office never go ungratified. Candour obliges me to say that some of them respect your friend, and I am persuaded would not wittingly be concerned in a plot against him; but they ''want the honour to defend.'' In all such junctures there are prompters and actors, accommodators, candle snuffers, shifters of scenes and mutes.''

The postscript to this same letter, written after a discussion on Washington's recommendation for a Quarter Master General, was even stronger:

"His opinion treated with so much indecent freedom and levity as affected me exceedingly and convinced me that, your suspicious of a baneful influence are not unfounded.''

However, not all of Washington's recommendations were so blatantly ignored. At least one, pertaining to a York patriot whose services had proved uniquely valuable, was given prompt attention. This man was Major John Clark who, in 1775 had laid aside his law books and marched with Captain Doudel to Cambridge. He later served with distinction as Aide-de-

"Sir — I take the liberty of introducing Major John Clark, the bearer of this, to your notice...''

camp to Major General Greene. But it was at Germantown that Clark's remarkable ability to obtain enemy intelligence brought him to the attention of Washington, who immediately gave him free rein in the area of espionage.

Major Clark soon organized an almost perfect spy ring operating out of Philadelphia. Of all his agents, old women, farmers, peddlers, even Philadelphians with supposedly strong British connections, not one was ever caught or executed. For three months after the occupation, he had watched every move the British made, often riding 20 to 60 miles a day to contact his agents. Clark's advance intelligence enabled the Americans to escape surprise attacks at Fort Mifflin and Fort Mercer on the Delaware in time to salvage their stores and scuttle their shipping. His warning saved Washington from a similar surprise at White Marsh and it was his knowledge of Howe's troop concentration at Darby that decided Washington against what have been a disastrous attack.

When, in January, an old wound suffered shortly before Brandywine, forced him to return to York, he carried a letter of introduction from Washington to Laurens. In response to Washington's strong endorsement of his capabilities to carry out any duties Congress might assign to him, Clark was appointed to the newly created post of Auditor, to audit and settle the public accounts of the main army.

Although this assignment was not to his liking, Clark somewhat reluctantly accepted it and carried out his duties, at great personal sacrifice, for two years. But in commenting on the affair some years later, Major Clark make this revealing observation: "At this critical period there were parties against that great officer (Washington) and it was known I was one of his warmest friends."

Major Clark knew that Col. Laurens and Lafayette knew — what every officer and common soldier at Valley Forge knew: General Washington was under fire.

Lafayette, who shared Washington's dislike of Conway and who was especially sensitive to any real or implied threat to his Chief, voiced his fears in a letter to Laurens. The President of Congress, writing with the wisdom and understanding born of his own experience with factions, endeavored to put events into their proper perspective. He patiently explained to the young Frenchman the role of parties as "The Sinews of Liberty", stressing how differences so extreme as to threaten dissolution, will suddenly unite to form a coalition in the face of a common enemy.

"Concerning the particular influences you speak of", he continued, "I must acknowledge your conjectures are not ill-founded. But I think the friends of our brave and virtuous General may rest assured that he is out of the reach of his Enemies, if he has an Enemy, a fact in which I am in doubt of. I believe I hear most that is said and know the outlines of almost all that has been attempted, but the whole amounts to little more than tittle tattle, which would be too much honoured by repeating it."

But what may have been "tittle tattle" on January 12 (the date of Laurens' letter) was to be regarded more seriously before the month was out.

The adulation of Gates was dangerously approaching the idolatry against which John Adams had warned Congress in 1776 after Washington's coup at Trenton. A similar "disposition to idolize an image" was to be found in some of the extravagant congratulatory messages written by members of Congress: For example:

> James Duane to Gates: "A Series of Victories so critical and decisive cannot fail of producing, with the Blessing of Heaven, the most Important and permanent advantages to the united States; while they have rescued this devoted Government, already almost ruined, from total Destruction.

> James Lovell to Gates: "How much you are to be envied my dear General! How different your Conduct and your Fortune! You have saved our Northern Hemisphere, and in spite of your Consummate and repeated Blundering, you have changed the Constitution of the Southern Campaign on the part of the Enemy from Offensive to Defensive."

It was in this rarified atmosphere that Gates made his triumphal entry into York, January 19, 1778. "A pleasant village", he found it, where he "was received with demonstrations of joy."

Gates immediately assumed his duties as President of the Board of War. Meeting with General Mifflin, Colonel Pickering and Richard Peters, the newly appointed civilian member, they rushed a plan through Congress for an immediate expedition into Canada. Without consulting Washington, Congress followed the recommendations of the Board by placing Lafayette in charge of the "irruption" and naming Conway as his second in command.

Expedition to Canada

This action which combined an insult to Washington with the folly of placing two commanders from a foreign country at the head of a military

General Horatio Gates
1727-1806

"Your name, Sir, will be
written in the breasts of the
grateful Americans of the
present Age and sent down
to posterity in characters
which will remain indelible
when the Gold (medal) shall
have chang'd its
appearance."
Henry Laurens
(the medal ordered by
Congress in York Town was
not delivered to Gates until
ten years later.)

operation, also detached Lafayette from Washington's staff, making him directly responsible to Gates.

This was no "tittle tattle"! Lafayette, young and ambitious, was eager for a command of his own, but not under these conditions. Upon receiving word of his appointment, he immediately talked with Washington and then protested to President Laurens: "How can I support the society of a man (Conway) who has spoken of my friend (Washington) in the most insolent and abusive terms, who tried to spread the fire in every part of the Army and the Country?"

It was bad enough to take orders from Gates, but the thought of Conway was insupportable. He would either choose his own subordinates or he would return to France. And he determined to deliver his ultimatum in person. Accordingly, instead of leaving for Albany, where the expedition was to be mobilized, Lafayette rushed off to York.

Meanwhile, during the period between the January 19th arrival of Gates and the February 2nd arrival of Lafayette, both Gates and Conway were attempting to convince Washington that the offending reference to a "weak general" had never appeared in their correspondence. Three times Conway had called on President Laurens proposing to publish his original letter, but was dissuaded on the grounds that such misunderstanding between Generals should be kept secret from the Enemy. His letter to Washington, branding the passage as a forgery, remained unanswered; but to Gates, who had written in a similar vein, shifting the blame to Wilkinson, Washington addressed a sarcastic reply, filled with censure and disbelief.

President Laurens, who by this time had seen the controversial letter, maintained a public silence, but admitted in private correspondence: "It is true Genl. Washington was misinformed. The letter does not contain the words which had been reported, but ten times worse in every view." The excerpt which he copied and later forwarded to Washington shows the difference in wording but the similarity of sentiment:

> "What a pity there is but one Gates! But the more I see of this army, the less I think it fit for general action under its present chiefs and actual discipline. I speak to you freely and wish I could serve under you."

But far more vicious than any writings ever attributed to Conway was the anonymous paper found on the stairs of the Court House on January 26th and handed to Laurens as he was presiding over Congress. Dated Jan. 17 it was addressed to "the Honble the Presidt. of Congress and every Member thereof." Fortunately, the ever-cautious Laurens glanced at the contents before reading it aloud, and when he saw it was an unsigned diatribe against Washington, he thrust it into his pocket, dismissing it with the comment that the hearth was the only proper depository for such an anonymous production.

"The Paper on the Stairs"

This three page paper entitled THE THOUGHTS OF A FREEMAN, contained 45 charges against Washington worthy of congressional investigation. Its concluding paragraphs were worded in much the same language employed by John Adams in his previous warnings against demigods:

> "That the people of America have been guilty of Idolatry by making a man their god — and that the God of Heaven and Earth will convince them that he is only a man.

> That no good may be expected from the standing army until Baal and his worshipers are banished from the camp."

Even to Laurens, who steadfastly maintained that no individual or group of individuals could depose Washington, this "paper on the stairs" was evidence that such forces were at work. Instead of consigning it to the hearth, he forwarded it the next day to Washington, calling it "an attempt for which I lack a proper Stigma."

Shortly after coming to York, General and Mrs. Gates were comfortably installed in a well-appointed house on West Market Street next door to the Golden Plough Tavern. Here they entertained their friends, and here Lafayette was invited to dine on the evening of his arrival. Present day visitors to the restored "Gates House" are shown the Banquet Room where Lafayette, on that occasion, blasted all hopes which might have been entertained of winning his support against Washington by proposing what has been termed "The Toast That Saved the Nation". Knowing full well the sentiments of his host and other guests — most likely the Board of War and the anti-Washington faction of Congress — Lafayette interpreted the omission of a toast to the Commander-in-Chief as a calculated insult. He, therefore, raised his own glass and, according to his memoirs, "brabbled the whole party and threw them into confusion by making them drink to the health of their General".

"After the sacrifices I have made, I have the right to expect two favors: one is to serve at my own expense, the other is to serve, at first, as volunteer...
I wish to serve near the person of General Washington till such time as he may think proper to entrust me with a division of the Army."
Marquis de Lafayette 1777

To claim that Lafayette's dramatic gesture broke the back of the Cabal would be a gross exaggeration. But it is significant that the very next day General Gates called on President Laurens expressing a sudden desire to be on "friendly terms with our great and Good General!" Also on that same day, February 3rd, under Lafayette's threat to return to France and take the foreign officers with him, Congress acceded to his demands. Even though Conway had already left for Albany, it was agreed that he be replaced by either General McDougal or the Baron de Kalb, to be appointed directly by Washington.

There can be little doubt that Lafayette's whirlwind visit of 36 hours had dealt the Cabal a serious blow.

But before the final curtain, there was one more dramatic scene to be enacted in York Town. The principals were Gates and Wilkinson. The young officer whose indiscretion had first uncovered the Cabal, had spend most of the intervening time with the northern army at Albany, unaware that Gates had denounced him as the betrayer of Conway's letter. Early in February on learning of his appointment as Secretary to the Board of War, he left Albany for York, traveling by sleigh as far as Reading, where he discovered that his old friend and commander was using him as a scapegoat in the whole unsavory affair. From Lancaster Wilkinson dispatched a note to Gates in which he demanded "satisfaction for his wounded honour" and the next day received a curt reply that any satisfaction he demanded would be forthcoming. Arriving in York at twilight on February 23rd, Wilkinson persuaded Lt. Colonel Ball of the Virginia Line to deliver his formal challenge:

Wilkinson — the Scapegoat

> "Sir:—
>
> *I have discharged my duty to you and my conscience. Meet me tomorrow morning behind the Episcopal Church, and I will then stipulate the satisfaction which you have promised to grant."*

An Affair of Honor

The next morning at 8 o'clock the 20 year old Wilkinson and the 48 year old Gates kept their appointment. But, like the Cabal itself, there was much talk and no action. Captain Stoddard, a mutual friend, acted as mediator, and Gates, unarmed, protested with tears of affection (?) that he "could not injure his own child".

After assurances by Gates that Conway had addressed much harsher sentiments to Washington's face than were exposed in his letter, Wilkinson professed "satisfaction", and the affair was over before it began.

The Duel Averted

All in all February 24th was a lucky day for Horatio Gates. Not only had Wilkinson agreed to call off the duel, but on that same day Washington expressed his willingness to end the controversy — to bury their past differences "in silence and, as far as future events will permit, oblivion."

The General concluded his letter with the statement:

> *"My temper leads me to peace and harmony with all men. And it is particularly my wish to avoid any personal feuds or dissensions with those who are embarked in the same great national interest with myself, as every difference of this kind must in its consequences be very injurious."*

After that, the Cabal died a slow but natural death. The Canadian expedition was a fiasco. Lafayette, disillusioned and chagrined, returned to Washington's command at Valley Forge. Mifflin, in difficulties with the Quarter Master Department, went back to Reading. In April Gates, replaced as President of the Board of War, was assigned to protect the Hudson River Forts under Washington. In late Spring, Conway, protesting his innocence and devotion to Washington to the end, returned to France.

The Conway Cabal was ended. In its course careers were ruined, dreams were shattered, reputations tarnished and friendships broken... truly, " a tale told by an idiot."

However, the weak and divided Congress would soon prove to itself and to the world the truth of Laurens' statement to Lafayette that factions, no matter how extreme, could unite against a common Enemy. This Congress, assembled in the Court House at York Town, was about to face "its finest hour."

The Voice of Courage

A Cry of Defiance

9

In the biography of a building, as in the life-story of a person, the inter-relationship of people and events, the variety of activities and incidents occurring simultaneously, defy any precise chronological order.

At the same time the Court House was buzzing with sub-rosa speculations on the Conway controversy, Congress was officially coping with the pressing problem of reorganizing, reforming and regulating the army. In late December Washington had written of its deplorable state and had urged the appointment of a committee "to repair immediately to camp... and with the commanding officer, or a committee of his appointment, prepare and digest the most perfect plan that can be devised for correcting all abuses and making new arrangements."

To Washington's enemies in Congress here was an opportunity to discredit him even further, or, at the very least, in the words of James Lovell, "To rap a Demi-G over the knuckles." The first three appointees to this crucial committee were all known to be of the anti-Washington faction: Dana of Massachusetts, Folsom of New Hampshire, and Joseph Reed of Pennsylvania. On January 12th John Harvie of Virginia was added to the committee, and three members of the Board of War, not yet arrived in York, were also appointed: Gates, Mifflin and Pickering.

A link between the Cabal and the committee personnel is established by a little known story recounted in William Dunlap's "History of the New Netherlands", published in 1840, and retold in "The Life of Lord Stirling" by his grandson, William Alexander Duer.

According to these accounts, a day had actually been appointed by the Cabal in Congress to nominate a committee to proceed to Valley Forge for the purpose of arresting Washington. Of the two New York delegates whose votes were needed to block this action, William Duer was seriously ill. A third delegate, young Gouverneur Morris, was known to be en route, but when he had not arrived on the morning of the appointed day, Duer determined to join his colleague, Francis Lewis, in the Court House.

Dr. Jones, the Virginia delegate, who was in attendance, warned his patient that such a move could prove fatal, but Duer replied: "Very Well, Sir, you have done your duty and I will do mine. Prepare a litter for me — if you refuse — someone else shall — but I prefer your care in this case."

Fortunately, the timely arrival of Morris prevented this sacrifice. When he and Lewis went to Duer's quarters, they found him on the litter, covered with blankets, attended by his physician and carriers, prepared to make what might have been his final journey. But with the opposition of New York, the Cabal faction lost its majority and the matter was dropped.

York Town, June 20, 1778

"Mr. G. Morris from N. York is an eternal speaker, and for artifice a 'Duane', and for brass, equal to any I am acquainted with."
Josiah Bartlett to William Whipple

Gouverneur Morris 1752-1816

This dramatic incident may or may not have been one of the factors which determined the request of the triumvirate, Gates, Mifflin and Pickering, to be excused from the Valley Forge assignment. Certain it is they knew the Conway affair had been recently exposed, they knew the contempt with which Conway's visit as inspector general had been received, and the plans for the Canadian expedition demanded their immediate attention at York Town. As a result, Charles Carroll of Maryland and 26 year old Gouvernor Morris were appointed in their stead.

Washington could have asked for no better advocate than Gouverneur Morris, who championed his cause with unflagging zeal and unfailing brilliance. His personal loyalty, his friendship with Lafayette (six years his junior) his grasp of the organizational problems besetting the army and his compassion for the common soldier made him the ideal liaison between camp and Congress. Almost immediately, he persuaded Dana and the rest of the committee that Washington's failures were due to lack of supplies rather than to lack of competence and by the sheer force of his own convictions was able to convince others — even Congress.

The condition of the army "naked, starving, out of health and out of spirit" demanded immediate reforms in the Quarter-master and Commissary Departments. By March, Nathaniel Greene had assumed the duties of Quarter-Master General, replacing Mifflin who, rightly or wrongly, received much of the blame for the sorry state of affairs.

Working with Washington and his staff, the army committee slowly hammered out a table of organization which, for the first time, defined the composition of Battalions and Companies within the Infantry, Artillery and Cavalry, also stipulating the number of commissioned and non-commissioned officers, their duties, rations, rate of pay and methods of promotion. This long overdue plan of organization, adopted by Congress on May 27th, was printed by order of that body, on the Hall and Sellers Press, as THE ESTABLISHMENT OF THE AMERICAN ARMY... another "FIRST" in the annals of the Court House at York Town.

But no "paper plan" however wise or far-reaching could miraculously transform Washington's starving, dispirited troops into a well disciplined professional army. This "Mission Impossible" was to be accomplished by a flamboyant, but imposing Prussian officer who arrived in York, February 5, 1778 with the highest recommendations from Silas Deane and Benjamin Franklin. His name was Frederick William Augustus Henry Ferdinand, Baron von Steuben.

Although introduced as a Lieutenant General of 22 years' experience with the King of Prussia, Von Steuben was actually a penniless captain, dropped from the service of Frederick The Great some fourteen years before; but his military knowledge and abilities were not in the least exaggerated.

Both Washington and Congress had good reason to be wary of foreign volunteers. Von Steuben's advance letters from Boston, declaring his sole ambition to be the honor of serving the American cause, with no other favor than to be received as a brother officer and "to deserve the title of a citizen of America" were suspiciously similar to the initial overtures of Conway. But Congress accepted his offer whole-heartedly and was not disappointed.

After remaining in York for thirteen days, the self-styled Baron and his entourage of two aides, one of whom was his seventeen year old French interpreter, and two servants, reported to Valley Forge. The arrival of the stout, middle-aged German, "resplendent in a new blue uniform upon whose breast blazed the dazzling jeweled Star of the Order of Fidelity of Baden" must have been something of a shock to Washington. But the man was a God-Send.

"Resolved that the president present the thanks of Congress to Baron Steuben for the zeal he has shown for the cause of America, and the disinterested tender of his military talents; and inform him that Congress cheerfully accepts of his service as a volunteer in the Army of these states."
York Town, Jan. 14, 1779

Baron von Steuben
1730-1794

A natural showman and a born teacher, Von Steuben became one of the few drill-masters in history to command the affection as well as the respect of his men. Unable to speak a word of English, he bullied, cajoled, and swore at his raggle-taggle Continentals through an interpreter. Since there were no army regulations, he wrote his own in French which were

110

then translated and finally prepared for distribution by John Laurens and Alexander Hamilton.

But the real secret of Von Steuben's success was his uncanny ability to understand the American mind.

"In the first place", he wrote to an old comrade, "the genius of this nation is not in the least to be compared with that of the Prussians, Austrians or French. You say to your soldier, 'Do this', and he doeth it, but I am obliged to say 'This is the reason why you ought to do it', and then he does it."

Congress had gambled on Von Steuben and won, but not every gamble paid off so handsomely. Earlier, in 1777 a half-mad Frenchman, Pierre Landais, had persuaded Silas Deane to recommend him for a Naval command. On his first ocean voyage he quelled a mutiny on board his ship the FLAMMAND, and in May of 1778 Congress granted him a monetary reward and sustained his rank of captain. The following year as captain of the frigate ALLIANCE, he perpetrated an act of infamy, unsurpassed in the history of the United States Navy. On the night of September 23, 1779, while supposedly assisting John Paul Jones in his famous engagement off Flamborough Head, Landais suddenly circled the BONHOMME RICHARD and the British SERAPIS, locked together in a death struggle, and mistakenly fired three broadsides from the ALLIANCE into the already crippled and rapidly sinking RICHARD.

"With regard to military discipline, I may safely say no such thing existed . . . the formation of the regiments was as varied as their mode of drill."
Baron von Steuben 1778

111

However, the brilliant services performed by such devoted men as Lafayette, Charles Armand, Thaddeus Koskiusco, Count Casimir Pulaski and Baron Von Steuben more than made up for the base actions committed by the free-booters and adventurers from foreign shores who used the cause of liberty for their own aggrandizement.

Spring Migration   Even as the men at Valley Forge were marching through the mud with more spirit and responding to Von Steuben's relentless roars with greater precision, the Solons at York Town sensed a gradual lifting of the heavy atmosphere, a faint stirring of the stale air in their Court House quarters. They were now approaching the season, described in a letter from Lovell to Samuel Adams, as the time "when certain birds of passage return who seldom appear in our flock during the winter."

There were arrivals and departures. There were new faces and new voices. At the end of January Thomas McKean arrived to represent the long silent state of Delaware. Samuel Huntington and Dr. Oliver Wolcott appeared at the Connecticut table. Dr. Nathaniel Scudder added his support to New Jersey. Robert Morris of Pennsylvania arrived in March, and Samuel Chase, on leave since October, returned from Maryland. Thomas Adams and John Bannister were spring replacements from Virginia. Dr. Thomas Burke took the North Carolina chair left vacant by John Penn and from South Carolina came John Matthews, Richard Huston and William Henry Drayton.

But despite the moderation of outdoor temperatures, there was no spring thaw of the one frozen issue which separated two opposing factions like a giant iceberg. This was Washington's proposal, relayed to Congress through the Army Committee, of a measure providing for half pay for life to the officers of the army. The proponents of the measure pointed to the alarming rate at which officers were resigning their commissions, on the slightest grounds, in favor of more lucrative employment. Since increased salaries would mean increased inflation with a further devaluation of currency, they argued that such an offer would prove a deterrent to resignations, which, too often, were occurring at the mere suggestion of disciplinary action.

The opposition questioned the power of Congress to create such an establishment and emphasized the potential dangers of creating a standing army, an evil not to be tolerated in their concept of a free and independent nation.

112

It was not until May 15th that this, "the most painful and disagreeable question that hath ever been agitated in Congress", was finally settled by compromise. Washington's officers would receive the added incentive of half pay, but for a period of seven years after the war, rather than for life.

While Congress at York Town was deadlocked over the half pay issue, three thousand miles away, in London, Lord North and Parliament were coming to grips with the bitter truth of William Pitt's prophecy of November 18th: "I know that the conquest of English America is an impossibility! You cannot conquer America!"

In December, after the news of Saratoga had reached England, Pitt sounded another warning to conciliate before the contemplated French alliance could be completed, but the old man was shouted down. However, in February, when the alliance had become an accomplished fact, a fact as yet unknown in America, Lord North conceded defeat by requesting the appointment of commissioners to sue for peace on the best possible terms.

"The only army you have in America may, by this time, be no more... I contend that we have not, nor can procure, any force sufficient to subdue America. It is monstrous to think of it."
Wm. Pitt. Earl of Chatham

The draft of Lord North's speech did not reach the United States until April. When Washington first read it, he considered it a hoax, but a dangerous hoax, designed to "poison the minds of our people and detach the wavering at least from our cause." He immediately forwarded a copy to Congress with the request that the "ablest pens be set to work to counteract its influence."

The reaction of Congress was as indignant as it was united. With one voice that hitherto "weak and divided" body denounced North's proposal to "forgive and forget" as a "piece of wicked and diabolical baseness." There was no lack of "able pens" to unmask the "wickedness and insincerity" of the enemy offer. Samuel Chase addressed his sentiments to the Governor of Maryland on April 20th:

> *"Gen. Howe has sent out of Philadelphia a Cart loaded with Hand Bills, expressing to be A Draught of a Bill to declare the Intentions of Parliament concerning the Right of imposing Taxes, within the Colonies. Two opinions prevail here. Some that this insidious scheme originated in Philadelphia, others the far greater Number believe it came from the Ministry. The manifest intention is to Amuse us with a Prospect of Peace and to relax our Preparations. I hope my Countrymen will have too much good sense to be deceived."*

And in a later post script he added: "I did intend Home, but I believe I shall stay and see it out. The Hour to try the Firmness and prudence of Man is near at Hand."

When, two days later, Henry Laurens took his accustomed place on the presidential dais, he must have noted a new determination on the faces of his colleagues assembled to deal with a proposition which could "prove more dangerous to their cause than 10,000 of the enemy's best troops."

But Gouverneur Morris, Francis Dana and William Henry Drayton had employed their "able pens" with a skill and daring which translated a proposal of peace into a renewed declaration of war — a second call to arms.

They interpreted the British tender of pardon as an implication of criminality in America's justifiable resistance, reasoning that to treat under it would be an implied acknowledgement of their status as rebels.

Of the possibility of treating with private individuals, they warned: "Any man, or body of men, who should presume to make any separate or partial convention or agreement with commissioners under the Crown of Great Britain . . . ought to be considered and treated as open and avowed enemies of these United States.

And, finally, the ultimatum:

"The Committee beg leave to report it as their opinion, that these United States cannot, with propriety, hold any conference or treaty with any commissioners on the part of Great Britain, unless they shall, as a preliminary thereto, either withdraw their fleets and armies, or else, in positive and express terms, acknowledge the independence of the said states.

And, inasmuch as it appears to be the design of the enemies of these states to lull them into a fatal security, to the end that they may act with a becoming weight and importance, it is the opinion of your committee that the several states be called upon to use the most strenuous exertions to have their respective quotas of continental troops in the field as soon as possible, and that all the militia of the said states may be held in readiness to act as occasion may require."

After the report was read and debated by paragraphs, there was a brief silence, but Laurens could detect no wavering glances as they watched Secretary Thomson complete the day's entry with a steady hand:

"Resolved unanimously That Congress approve and confirm the said report.

Ordered, that the same be published."

For the 26 men present in the York Court House on April 22, 1778 there could be no finer hour. By their unanimous action they had totally

114

committed themselves and their country, already on the edge of financial and military disaster, to upholding their independence as proclaimed in Philadelphia July 4, 1776. From that day on there could be no turning back. It was independence or nothing.

It was apparent to Congress that Lord North's sudden and uncharacteristic proposal to Parliament had been induced by fear of French intervention. Hopefully, the fair wind from France was blowing in the right direction. Ten days later these hopes were confirmed by the glorious news of the French Alliance.

About three o'clock on Saturday afternoon, May 2, 1778, after Congress had adjourned for the weekend, the clanging of the Court House bell brought the members rushing from nearby taverns and more distant lodgings, to welcome Simeon Deane just arrived from Paris with the long awaited dispatches. *News from France*

The terse entry in the Journal for that date hardly does justice to the drama of the scene!

> *"Congress was convened and the despatches laid before them. Among which a treaty of commerce and alliance, concluded between the king of France and the United States of America on the 6 February last."*

There they were ... priceless documents (at least the authentic French and English copies) — conceived and signed at the brilliant court of Versailles, now spread out on the tables of a small Pennsylvania court room. No tablets of gold could have been more precious:

> *THE TREATY OF AMITY AND COMMERCE, guaranteeing perpetual peace and friendship, and establishing unrestricted trade on the basis of "the most perfect equality and reciprocity."*

> *THE TREATY OF ALLIANCE, pledging mutual assistance against Great Britain, and specifically dedicated to "maintain effectually the liberty, sovereignty and independence, absolute and unlimited of the United States."*

There is no record of how soundly the Congress slept that night, but more than one devout, night-capped delegate must have evoked the blessings of Heaven on the wily old statesman in the steel spectacles, who had captured Paris so much more completely and effectively that ever Howe and his army had captured Philadelphia.

During the Monday sessions, as the documents were read and reread, Congress grew more and more impressed with the "magnanimity and generosity shown by His Most Christian Majesty. Satisfied that there was nothing ''which indicates any Design of obtaining any Advantage over us', and pleased by being treated ''As if we were in the plentitude of power and in the greatest security'', Congress unanimously ratified both treaties, on condition of two minor changes subsequently approved by France.

Such are the strange contrivances of Fate that both the first and final treaties of the war should be identified with YORK. The Paris building where Franklin, Jay and Adams signed the ''Definitive Treaty of Peace'', recognizing the Independence of the United States, September 3, 1783, was THE HOTEL YORK

But the general rejoicing over the French treaties was of broader and deeper dimensions than the ''illuminations'' at York Town and the grand ''feu de joie'' which so delighted Lafayette at Valley Forge. There was an awakening spirit of national pride and a re-dedication to the war effort. ''America has now taken her rank among the Nations'', wrote Samuel Chase, ''and has it in her power to secure her liberty and independence. Let us be grateful to our God for this singular mark of his favor and protection and continue to exert every means in our power to support the war.''

Congress wisely decided to use the good news from France as a launching pad for a direct appeal to the public for stiffer resistance and further sacrifice in the crucial days ahead. A committee was appointed, consisting of Richard Henry Lee, Samuel Chase and Gouverneur Morris to prepare ''An Address of the Congress to the Inhabitants of the United States of America''.

Although written largely by Morris, in the grandiloquent style of the day, there were no false promises of a quick or easy victory. Morris reminded them of past sufferings — the horrors of Indian raids, the mistreatment of prisoners; he cautioned them against further false overtures for peace at the price of honor and liberty; he warned them to expect "one severe conflict", stating flatly "Your foreign alliances, though they secure your independence, cannot secure your country from desolation; "He advocated a tight program of economy and self denial; he encouraged them by contrasting their past weakness with their new-found strength, but hammered away at the central theme: "Arise then! to your tents, and gird you for the battle!"

This remarkable piece of rhetoric, which was to be read by ministers of all denominations after divine service in all places of public worship, concluded with the exhortation:

> *"Above all, bring forward your armies into the field. Trust not to appearances of peace or safety. Be assured that, unless you preserve, you will be exposed to every species of barbarity. But, if you exert the means of defence which God and nature have given you, the time will soon arrive when every man shall sit under his own vine and fig tree, and there shall be none to make him afraid."*

In York Town this address was translated into German and read to the German-speaking congregations in that lauguage on Sunday, the 24th of May.

In Congress spirits were high and hopes as bright as the summer sunshine streaming through the Court House windows. Lord Howe, whose occupation of Philadelphia had been more of a social than a military triumph, had resigned and been replaced by Sir Henry Clinton. Rumours of an early evacuation were growing stronger every day.

Philip Livingston
"Eminently distinguished for his talents and rectitude."

But before such rumors could materialize, Congress lost one of its most respected and able members, Philip Livingston. The 65 year old Livingston, already in failing health, had made the long trip from New York on horseback, and never recovered from the journey. In spite of the care of the physicians who were his fellow congressmen, he died within a month of his arrival, and was buried in the early evening of June 12th in the German Reformed Churchyard. As was the custom, Congress attended the funeral in a body and declared a one month period of official mourning. Services were conducted by Chaplain Duffield with members of the York clergy also in attendance. Some years later his grandson, Stephen Van Rensselaer, erected a suitable monument in his memory which still marks his final resting place in Prospect Hill Cemetery.

The day after Livingston's funeral, Congress received a packet of letters signed by Lord North's Peace Commissioners, William Eden, George Johnstone and the Earl of Carlisle. From the moment of their arrival in Philadelphia, earlier in the month, this delegation had found little to encourage them. Washington had promptly refused to grant them safe conduct through his lines, nor would he permit their secretary, Dr. Ferguson, to deliver their messages in person. When the papers finally reached Congress on June 13th, they met with almost instant rejection.

President Laurens had barely begun to read the first communication, when an unfortunate reference to the French alliance as "the insidious interposition of a power which has, from the first settlement, been actuated with enmity to us both", halted the proceedings. Congress refused to listen to "offensive language against his most Christian Majesty!"

Although the letters were read in their entirety a few days later, the Congress of June 17th was even more belligerent in their opposition than the Congress on April 22nd. Stronger in numbers, they were also supported by a powerful ally, and fortified with the knowledge that Washington's army, thanks to Baron von Steuben, now Inspector General, was an effective fighting force.

The following indignant reply from the President of Congress ended all hope of negotiation:

"I have received the letter from your excellencies of the 9th instant, with the enclosures, and laid them before Congress. Nothing but an earnest desire to spare the effusion of human blood could have induced them to read a paper containing expressions so disrespectful to his most Christian majesty, the good and great ally of these states, or to consider propositions so derogatory to the honor of an independent nation.

The acts of the British parliament, the commission from your sovereign, and your letter, suppose the people of these states to be subjects of the Crown of Great Britain, and are founded on the idea of dependence, which is utterly inadmissable.

I am further directed to inform your excellencies that Congress are inclined to peace, notwithstanding the unjust claims from which this war originated, and the savage manner in which it hath been conducted. They will, therefore, be ready to enter upon the consideration of a treaty of peace and commerce not inconsistent with treaties already subsisting, when the king of Great Britain shall demonstrate a sincere disposition for that purpose. The only solid proof of this disposition will be an explicit acknowledgment

of the independence of these states, or the withdrawing of his fleets and armies."

Upon receipt of this summary dismissal of their proposals and the consistent rejection of their secret attempts to create individual defection by bribes and promises, the Commission finally admitted failure. The entire mission, in the words of Washington had been "ridiculously mortifying."

But even more mortifying to British pride was the forced withdrawal of General Clinton's army from Philadelphia. Congress received the news from Washington that the coast was finally clear, on June 20th and promptly ordered "that the Boards of Congress put themselves in readiness to move from this place."

It was a hectic time of packing and sorting, winding up personal affairs, paying bills and dealing with official business which included a reopening of discussions on the Articles of Confederation and drafting a proper form for their ratification. Newly arrived members barely had time to unpack before they were repacking for the journey to Philadelphia scheduled for June 27th. Dr. Samuel Holton of Massachusetts recorded the week's proceedings in his diary:

> *"June 19: Being somewhat indisposed and not having proper lodgings, I did not take my seat in Congress. We are informed by Gen. Washington that the Enemy have left the City of Philadelphia and our people have taken possession. The people here are not at all obliging. I want to git from this house.*
>
> *June 20: I have not taken my seat in Congress for the reasons mentioned yesterday.*
>
> *June 21: Sabbath day being somewhat indisposed did not attend public worship.*
>
> *June 22: I took my seat in Congress and it is a very august assembly.*
>
> *June 23: Attended in Congress and the chief of the day was taken up in disputing on the Articles of Confederation.*
>
> *June 24: Attended in Congress, dined with the President.*
>
> *June 25: Attended in Congress. Toward night I walked out with a number of gentlemen of Congress about a mile to a farmhouse. The people was kind, we eat Cherries and drank whiskey.*
>
> *June 26: Attended in Congress and it is the hottest day I ever knew. Went and drank with the President and drank tea with the Secretary.*

June 27: Congress adjourned to the City of Philadelphia to meet on Thursday next, 10 o'clock."

The whole manner of their departure was just as devoid of ceremony and emotion as Holton's matter-of-fact account. They packed their bags, paid their bills (one of which was the sum of 36 dollars to Martin Breneise for his services at the Court House plus another 9 12/90 for ringing the bell) and left!

Nine months ago these men of Congress had arrived in York, a weary, dejected and defeated lot. Now, on this busy June Market Day, they were leaving in full confidence that victory, though neither quick nor easy, would ultimately be theirs. They had lived to see the day "when, instead of Americans licking the dust from the feet of a British Minister, the tables had turned." And they had done the turning.

Somewhere in the train of baggage wagons, carefully packed and guarded, were the same priceless papers which John Adams had deemed of more importance than all the members of Congress. But to that treasured hoard had now been added a new set of "American Scriptures": The Articles of Confederation, the Convention of Saratoga with its related correspondence, and the Treaties with France.

None of the men who rode eastward on that summer day would ever see York Town again. But their names and their deeds were forever invisibly inscribed on the walls of the little Court House in the Square. In what other American building had so few done so much for so many — in so short a space of time?

Echoes of Greatness 10

To the people of York Town, gathered at the Court House on July 4th, 1778 for the ceremonial reading of the Declaration of Independence, the words must have been fraught with a deeper, richer meaning than on previous occasions. For nine months the priceless "Testament of Freedom" had been in their keeping, safely locked away inside the very building where they were assembled. For nine months they had rubbed elbows with the men most dedicated to its preservation. Together they had mingled their voices in prayers and hymns of thanksgiving for the protection and recognition of the new nation founded on its principles. They had willingly tightened their belts in anticipation of further sacrifices in its defense.

Small wonder it was recorded that: "The anniversary of the Declaration of Independence was celebrated here in a very joyful manner."

There was every reason for the people to rejoice. The winter was past. The crops looked good. The Red Coats had skedaddled out of Philadelphia, and five or six of Washington's lads, with food in their bellies and decent boots, could outfight a dozen Britishers any day!

As for the Court House, its doors and windows were wide open. No more secret meetings, no sergeant-at-arms, no candles burning far into the night, no more special messengers riding hell-for-leather right up to the Court House door! The little building, which they had come to regard with some degree of awe while it was occupied by the grim-faced Congress was no longer a Capitol, but merely the familiar county court house where a man could transact his business and pass the time of day with his friends and

neighbors. Soon the courts would reconvene, the Justices resume their rightful place, and the Commissioners would look after the affairs of the County which were in sore need of attention.

But the end of the war was not as close as many dared to believe. Five more Independence Day celebrations would take place before the British finally laid down their arms, and even then, life would never be quite so simple and uncomplicated as before. For York was now part of the national proving ground. In every Town Hall and Court House throughout the thirteen states, a new philosophy of government would soon be tested, a philosophy which would capture the imagination of the world.

By reason of its physical location, the Court House remained the center of activity. The building was linked to history by a long list of prepositions. Every important event took place AT-IN-NEAR-or-AROUND the Court House. Every noted personage went INTO it, passed BY it or THROUGH it. Every proclamation, message, or news bulletin was issued FROM it, BY it, or TO it!

York's "Foreign Legions"

A few of the more striking Court House-related personages and events stand out with a special, close-up clarity against the tapestry of time.

One is the dashing figure of General Casimir Pulaski who arrived in York in 1779 with a commission to recruit a legion of his own. Pulaski was a familiar visitor to the Court House, partly because of the frequent need for official intervention between his obstreperous dragoons and the populace. The story of his warm friendship with the York artist, John Fisher, who designed the Court House weathervane in his honor, has already been recounted.

Another is the debonair and charming Marquis De La Rouerie, better known as Brigadier General Charles Armand who, upon the death of Pulaski, assumed command of his legion, later redesignated as Armand's Partisan Corps. For eleven months before disbanding in 1783, Armand and his men were quartered in York. They were so highly regarded by the townspeople that a group of leading citizens met in the Court House, a few days before his departure, to compose a farewell letter, thanking him for his services to America and commending him on the deportment of his troops. Armand replied with true French gallantry:

> *"Permit me to say, gentlemen, that soldiers cannot be guilty of misconduct where the inhabitants are kind to them . . . I think it is my duty to thank you for the good behavior of the Legion whilst among you, for it was encouraged and supported by your conduct toward them."*

There is also the scene of the dramatic arrival of the fascinating Baroness Riedesell and her three small daughters in the Court House Square during the summer of 1779. Wife of General Freiderich Riedesell, commander of 2400 Hessian troops during the battle of Saratoga, the Baroness was technically a prisoner of war. But her luxurious style of travel, and the hospitality extended to her as she followed her captured husband from New York to Virginia and back again to a port of embarkation, would have befitted visiting royalty. Her journal, published in America in 1867 confirmed the suspicion entertained by Congress of at least one violation of the Saratoga Convention. In her book the Baroness boasted of having concealed the conquered German colors in a mattress which she managed to take with her and triumphantly return to her native land after her release in 1783.

Hessian Visitors

And finally, in this brief series of close-ups — the tragedy enacted outside the Moravian burial ground near Penn Common, on a bright May morning of 1781 — the execution of military prisoners court-martialed for inciting revolt within the Pennsylvania Line.

General (Mad) Anthony Wayne had arrived in York in February under orders to organize a march to Virginia in support of the hard-pressed southern army. For three months he had been forced to pay his troops with badly deflated Continental currency instead of the "hard money" promised him by the State. York tradesmen refused to accept this all but worthless paper, even for necessities, and some are said to have encouraged the soldiers to defy their orders and stand up for their rights. To what extent such dangerous advice contributed to the breakdown of discipline has never been determined, but the insubordination of the Line soon rose to an alarming extreme.

When the County Militia assembled for their regular muster on the parade ground, the mutineers broke up the exercise and forced them to disperse. Next came threats from the ringleaders to burn and plunder the town unless their demands were met. Secretly the officers organized a citizens' committee and spend one whole night in the Court House helping them prepare cartridges for their defense in case of attack.

Mutiny!

But the next morning the Revolt of the Pennsylvania Line came to a violent and bloody end.

Of the many accounts of this regrettable and relatively unpublicized affair, none is more vivid or more accurate than the report of the General who could understand but not condone a mutiny:

LETTER OF GENERAL ANTHONY WAYNE

May 20, 1781

"The day antecedent to that on which the march was to commence, a few leading mutineers on the right of each regiment, called out to pay them in REAL and not IDEAL money. They were not to be trifled with. Upon this, they were ordered to their tents, which being peremptorily refused, the principals were either knocked down, or confined by the officers who were previously prepared for this event. A Court-Matrial was ordered on the spot.,—the commission of the crime, trial and execution were all included in the course of a few hours in front of the line paraded under arms. The determined countenances of the officers produced a conviction to the soldiery that the sentence of the Court-Martial would be carried into execution at every risk and consequence. Whether by design or accident, the particular friends and messmates of the culprits were their executioners, and while the tears rolled down their cheeks in showers, they silently and faithfully obeyed their orders without a moment's hesitation. Thus was the hideous monster (mutiny) crushed in its birth, however, to myself and officers a most painful scene."

And a "painful scene" it remains to this day, when the names of the victims appear only in footnotes or are completely erased by time: "Macaroni Jack", one of the ringleaders whose wife served as a camp washerwoman . . . Jack Smith, a member of the line for only forty eight hours . . . and Sergeant Lilly described by his mates as "a fine fellow", "an excellent scholar". Most eye-witness accounts agree that a fourth man was put to death on that fatal morning, and that two others were unexpectedly and unexplainedly reprieved and returned to their companies, even while the troops were still marching and counter-marching past the crumpled bodies of their companions.

York accepted the transition from National Capital to County Seat as easily and naturally as it accepted the transition from Sunday to Monday or April to May. The post-revolutionary role of the Court House was much the same as before. It remained the center of local government, the site of elections and the seat of Justice.

The Treaty of Paris in 1783, the adoption of the Constitution in 1787, even the election of George Washington as first President of the United States in 1789 made little alteration in manners and customs. But, nevertheless, in York County, as well as in every corner of America, the quality of life and the character of the people were gradually changing. The Revolution had left its mark. People were more conscious of their rights and quicker to defend them. They had willingly paid for their freedom with blood and sacrifice, but the new state and federal taxes levied to defray the actual cost of the war, frequently met with violent opposition.

In York, on one occasion, this opposition errupted into a full scale riot, humorously described in Glossbrenner's HISTORY OF YORK COUNTY as "The Cow Insurrection of 1786."

The facts of the case were simple. An Excise Officer had seized a cow belonging to John Bixler of Manchester Township with the purpose of selling it in lieu of taxes. But, on the day of the sale, as Glossbrenner tells it,

> "A company of about 100 men set out from the neighborhood of the poor animal's former residence, armed some with clubs, others with pistols or guns; and directing their march towards York, they crossed Chicken Bridge (at the end of North George Street) and, in single or Indian file, marched into town. Their captain, who was Godfrey King, led them on, with dread determination, to the place where her vaccine excellence was exposed to vendition. This was the square where Main and Beaver streets cross each other. The appearance of such a body of men so armed for outrage, was the subject of an instant alarm. They had barely proceeded to commit violence when the whole town, as on the alarm of fire, was assembled together."

In the free-for-all that followed, Colonel Henry Miller, aimed a blow at one of the rioters with such force that his sword imbedded itself about an inch into the wagon tongue over which his intended victim had leaped for safety. After a brief skirmish, the mob dispersed, a half dozen armed men were arrested, brought to trial and heavily fined.

As for the cow . . . Although the wrong man was punished for cutting the rope around her neck and turning her loose, there is no mention of her ultimate fate; Glossbrenner's tongue-in-cheek conclusion being that the whole affair "brought Manchester and York into a fond and loving union."

But the following year the Court House was the scene of a much more important event than the trial of the "cow-insurgents." On September 24th, 1787, by act of the General Assembly, York was incorporated as a Borough and a public meeting was held at the Court House for the election of officers. The men entrusted with administering the first municipal government were chosen mainly from the ranks of Revolutionary heroes. Colonel Henry Miller became the Chief Burgess with David Candler, a Lieutenant of

"The people, even to the lowest ranks, have become more attentive to their liberties, more inquisitive, about them, and more determined to defend them."

John Adams

"Her vaccine excellence"

the Flying Camp, as his assistant. On the Board of Burgesses were James Smith, Signer of the Declaration, Michael Doudel, Captain of the first Company of York Riflemen, and the distinguished Colonel David Grier. Also serving as Assistant Burgesses were Baltzer Spangler, well known tavern proprietor and captain in the militia, Christopher Lauman and Peter Mundorf. Both High Constable Christopher Stair and Town Clerk George Loeffler had served with the Flying Camp.

This spirit of patriotism which dominated the first municipal election was characteristic of the times. It was an age when people publicly demonstrated their love of country and seized every opportunity to honor its heroes. In those early years of the Republic no holiday could compare with the Fourth of July, and the ardor with which it was celebrated in York County is a matter of record.

In 1788 the Court House witnessed a dual celebration — the 12th anniversary of the Declaration of Independence and the first observance of the adoption of the Constitution of the United States.

On this occasion the military exercises in the Square were followed by an Industrial Parade and a banquet at which toasts were offered by representatives of more than forty different trades. Although toasts at banquets are not uncommon, these particular toasts, each one couched in the special language of a given occupation, were well worth preserving. Some of them reflect the Federal and Anti-Federal Conflict which was still obstructing the ratification of the Constitution:

NAILOR'S

"May the government be well pointed and have a good head."

BLACKSMITH'S

"May the thirteen states be welded into one united empire, by the hammer of conciliation on the anvil of peace; and may the men who attempt to blow the coals of discord be burned by the sparks."

WAGGON-MAKER'S

"Three more spokes to our new wheel — a federal band for its tire, a willing people for its axis—a political wisdom to set it in motion, and may its progress never be retarded by the lock chain of opposition."

TOBACCONIST'S

"May the leaves of anti-federalism be twisted together, and fastened by thorns, or be rolled into tubes, and end in a puff."

HOUSE-CARPENTER'S

"The new political mansion — may its compartments be commodious — May three rafters be added to the ten which already support its roof — and may the lights be great and many."

The "three rafters", the last three states to ratify, were added in 1789 and Washington was hailed as the first President of the United States. When, three years later, the great man elected to visit York during a tour of the southern states, the jubilation of the Borough knew no bounds.

Washington had passed this way when he was a young surveyor for Lord Fairfax, and would journey through the town again in 1794, but this visit of July 2-3, 1791 was the longest and most spectacular.

"An occaision of irrepressible joy!"

The Court House blazed with the light of forty one pounds of candles for which the County Commissioners paid the sum of fourteen dollars! Every detail of his brief visit has been recorded: how he was escorted into town by a delegation of citizens and two military companies; how his arrival was announced by the ringing of bells and the firing of cannon; how he walked about town with his friend, Colonel Hartley, then a member of the United States Congress, and later drank tea at the Colonel's home on West Market Street.

After spending the night at the hostelry of Baltzer Spangler, Jr., "Second door west of Court House Square", the President "was waited upon by the Chief Burgess and principal inhabitants" for a ceremonious exchange of formal courtesies.

The conclusion of this unforgettable occasion is described in Washington's diary:

"Received and answered an address from the inhabitants of Yorktown — & there being no Episcopal Minister present in the place, I went to 'hear morning Service performed in the Dutch reformed church — which, being in that language, not a word of which I understood, I was in no danger of becoming a proselyte to its religion by the eloquence of the Preacher.

After Service, accompanied by Colo Hartley & half a dozen other Gentlemen, I set off for Lancaster."

By the time of Washington's visit, the Country, with a population approaching 38,000, had outgrown its Court House. Over-crowding compelled the Commissioners to rent a meeting room in the home of David Candler on West Market Street until a new public building could be erected with adequate office space.

President George Washington 1732-1799

County Office Building of 1793 Drawn by Lewis Miller
Its torch-surmounted urns removed in 1814. Jacob Barnitz, wounded Revolutionary hero, in foreground

Drawn by Lewis Miller, 1796-1882

*Only known depiction of an
18th Century American
court house interior.
On bench: Judge Joseph
Henry, Jacob Rudisill,
Robinson and Glascow.*

Although the proposed building had been approved by the state legislature, no precise location had been specified. Therefore, when construction began in 1792 at a site east of the Court House, but within the boundaries of the square, objections were raised on the grounds of blocking a public highway. The Burgesses appealed to Colonel Thomas Hartley for a legal opinion. Although granting some merit to the opposition, and admitting that the location would not have been his personal choice, Hartley strongly advised against further delay. Thus by 1794 the imposing structure known as the State House or Public Office Building was completed.

Meanwhile the Court House itself had not been neglected. A spectators' gallery had been constructed inside the courtroom in 1793, and three years later it was completely renovated. The old courtroom was handsomely decorated in elaborate Georgian style. Some new tables and chairs

*1796 Doorway
Detail from L. Miller
drawing*
Courtesy of Hist. Soc. of York Co.

were purchased, and the space behind the Judges' Bench appropriately ornamented with the State Coat of Arms and a carved figure of Justice, both by John Fisher.

The "New Look of 1796" also extended to the entrance of the building with the construction of a pedimented door-frame, flanked by fluted columns of Corinthian design and lighted by a semi-circular transom. All in all, the Court House had taken on a grace and dignity well suited to its time and function.

"We shape our buildings", wrote Winston Churchill, "thereafter, they shape us." The Commissioners of 1754 had shaped the Court House in the established pattern of a provincial Seat of Justice, but thereafter, the building had shaped the community in a variety of ways.

The York County churches sustained the people's faith in God; the York County Court House sustained their confidence in government and law. By serving as a forum for political discussions and as a platform for visiting orators it helped mold public opinion. As the town's first library and place of public entertainment it contributed to York's intellectual and cultural development.

In 1794 The York County Library Company, with James Smith as President, published a list of 125 volumes stored on the second floor of the Court House. This collection, later moved to the Office Building, and still later transferred to the Golden Globe Inn on the Square, included works by Plato, Locke, Johnson and Franklin. This first library offered its services to the public at a fee of $2.00 per year.

Traveling theater troops were well received by York audiences who crowded into the Court House to see their various attractions ranging from Shakespeare to slap-stick. Congress is reported to have enjoyed a Shakespearean production during the winter of 1778, and the following advertisement of 1791, reprinted in "The Spengler Annals", shows the type of entertainment offered to "polish the Tastes, improve the Manners and Cultivate the Genius of the Rising Generation:"

> *"On Thursday evening the 17th instant, Mr. McGraths Company of Comedians, will open the Theatre at the Court House, elegantly and suitably prepared with the celebrated Tragedy*
>
> *OF DOUGLAS,*
>
> *(Written by The Rev. Doctor Home)*
>
> *Preceding the Play, A Moral defense of the Stage addressed to the United*

States, To be delivered by Mr. Fitzgerald, At the end of the Play a Humerous Dissertation on Jealousy, Mrs. McGrath, To which will be added a Comedy of three acts called,

BARNEBEY BRITTLE

A Wife At Her Wits End

The Doors to be opened at six, and the Curtain to raise at half past six O'Clock precisely — Tickets to be had at the Printing Office at Dunn's Tavern, and of Mr. McGrath,

No money will be taken at the Door

N. B. Mr. McGrath begs leave to observe, that not being lucky enough to see any of the Commissioners (of which John Spengler was one) previous to his sending the above Advertisement for Insertion, he has advertised it on the following principles — The Approbation of some very respectable Inhabitants, and his Design of appropriating the Profits of the Third Night's Exhibitions for the Benefit of any Public Purpose the Magistrates of the Town may choose to apply it. Tuesday Morning November 15 1791.''

But the real-life drama of the court room, the comedies and tragedies played out before Judge and Jury attracted even larger audiences than the fantasies of a make-believe world.

In 1797 the strange case of Dr. Dady drew a capacity crowd. Dr. Dady, a ''con-artist'' and imposter of the first order, had come to York County as a Hessian soldier. His fluency in both German and English had enabled to palm himself off among the more gullible inhabitants, first as a minister of the Gospel, then as a physician with super-natural powers. Preying on the superstitious beliefs of the country folk, Dady and his associates circulated the story of an enchanted treasure which would be divided among a select and favored few with the power to break the magic spell.

Dady's associates traveled through the county organizing different groups of victims who were then instructed by either a white or black ghost (played by one of their number) to purchase a vial of ''dulcimer elixir'' or ''Asiatic Sand'' from the good doctor. This ridiculous but highly ingenious scheme was so successful that some of the associates went into business for themselves. Their operations became so wide-spread that by the time the ring was broken up, trials were held in both York and Lancaster.

Judge John Joseph Henry, who presided over the York trial, which resulted in heavy fines and stiff prison sentences, reported witnesses

Nicholas Gelwix
High Sheriff 1800
Courtesy of Hist. Soc.
of York Co.

having paid as much as $121.00 for eleven ounces of the "eliximer" which was a compound of "copperas and cayenne pepper" mixed with a generous amount of "Hokum". So Justice prevailed, but not before the nefarious Dady had bilked scores of honest farmers out of their hard-earned savings.

Among the more sensational cases conducted in the Court House were two which had more serious, and far-reaching consequences.

In 1803 the trial and sentencing of Margaret Bradley for the attempted poisoning of Sabina and Matilda Bentz triggered what was headlined as "The Negro Conspiracy to Burn York." For three weeks serious fires of undetermined origins ravaged the town before the plot was discovered and the arsonists arrested.

In 1815 the murder of Robert Dunn at a Street Fair, for which three persons were convicted of manslaughter, prompted the grand jury to declare the fairs a public nuisance. The State Legislature of 1816 ordered the discontinuance of a custom which York had enjoyed since 1765.

As the "Little General" watched the celebration of "Shooting in the New Year" which marked the turn of the century, he had good reason to feel secure on his Court House perch. The building had survived the most troubled times of the Revolution. It had held its own through the first uncertain years of the new Republic, and aside from a few broken window panes and some scorched paint, had come unscathed through the destructive hail storn and disastrous fire of 1797. With its brave new front and interior renovations, it should be good for . . . at least another hundred years!

The first celebrity to visit York in the 19th Century was the second President of the United States. On May 29, 1800, John Adams, on his way from Philadelphia to Washington, where he would become the first Chief Executive to occupy the newly completed White House, revisited the town he had last seen twenty three years before.

But if the sight of the Court House recalled the struggle to unite the nation of which he was now the head, he gave no sign. If he recognized James Smith's Law Office where he had presided over the Board of War in 1777, or the Roberdeau House where he first learned of his proposed appointment to the Court of France, he made no comment. After a formal exchange of courtesies with Chief Burgess Atlee, in which he congratulated the people of York and Lancaster on their thrift and industry, their progress and patriotism, he rode away, accompanied by the respectful, if not

President John Adams
1735-1826

tumultuous applause of the people who had come to do him honor.

Within the next few decades the Court House would be a silent witness to many stirring events. During the War of 1812 the people would once again assemble to roll cartridges, and Captain Spangler's York Volunteers would march to the relief of Baltimore.

On a snowy February night in 1819, Major General Andrew Jackson made a brief appearance at Hammersley's Hotel (formerly Roberdeau's house) where people turned out in force to cheer the Hero of New Orleans. His sleigh having broken down outside of town, the General had arrived on foot, still fuming from an argument with his driver, reported to have made the air sulphurous with oaths! But he received his admirers with courtesy and, apparently warmed by their good will, proceeded on to Lancaster that same night.

But for sheer joy and excitement no event of the century could equal the visit of Lafayette in 1825. The beloved Frenchman, then making a tour of the 24 states as "The Guest of the Nation" had stopped briefly and unexpectedly on his way from Baltimore on January 29th. He was escorted to Harrisburg by a delegation of leading citizens and invited to return for a banquet given in his honor on February 2nd. His acceptance threw the town into a frenzy of preparation. There must be illuminations, there must be bands and bunting, even badges with steel engravings of the guest of honor were hastily prepared for the invited guests. The dining room at the Globe Inn was enriched by the addition of twelve elegant chairs from the finest homes in York and the table was set with the best silver and china available.

Lafayette!
The Toast of the Town!

When the General and his son, George Washington Lafayette, arrived, they were received with every military and civil honor the town could bestow. In an open barouche, driven by John Koons, the distinguished visitors toured the principal streets which were thronged with cheering spectators from all over the county.

Lafayette must have noticed many changes in the York Town he had known. The Square had been paved in 1814, and the Court House where he had received his commission as Major General, was now an imposing four-gabled structure boasting a tall tower with a Town Clock, the pride of the community.

To those attending the reception and banquet at the Globe, the event was the social highlight of their lives. They wrote of it in their journals, described it in their letters, and carefully preserved every momento for their

Courthouse, Market shed and Globe Inn

Drawing by Wm. Wagner circa 1830

descendants. A silk badge, a satin gown, a silver spoon or a china teapot associated with the occasion become an heirloom over night.

Although Mr. John Schmidt, cashier of the York Bank, enjoyed the distinction of being the only guest to address the General in his native tongue, there was no language barrier. David Prince, Principal of the York County Academy, said of him: "He speaks the English very readily, making use of good and appropriate language, tho' he has much of the French accent...He is very ready of access and makes every one easy in his company."

As Lafayette raised his glass in the exchange of toasts, he must have recalled another banquet, exactly 47 years ago to the day, February 2, 1778, when as a lad of twenty, he had "brabbled" a disloyal company by proposing the health of their commander-in-chief.

But this was another time and place. To the toast which hailed him as a "deliverer" and "Champion of Freedom", he responded:

> *"The Town of York, the seat of our American Union in our most gloomy time. May her citizens enjoy a proportionate share of American prosperity."*

York as it appeared at the time of Lafayette's visit February 2, 1825.

The wave of patriotism inspired by Lafayette's visit continued to sweep the country through the widely celebrated 50th Anniversary of Independence. On July 4th, 1826 some fifty veterans of the Revolution assembled at the south front of the Court House to hear an address by Charles Barnitz, orator of the day, and to receive the tributes of their friends and neighbors.

But throughout the nation the spirit of the Jubilee Year was considerably saddened by the loss of two great Americans. Thomas Jefferson had died at Monticello, shortly after midnight on the morning of that "Glorious Fourth", and John Adams, whose son was then President of the United States, survived his old friend and "dedicated opponent" by only a few hours.

One by one the old leaders of the Revolution, the Signers of the Declaration, the architects of the Articles of Confederation, and the fathers of the Constitution, were vanishing. Theirs was an age that was dying, "but a new one was coming to birth."

York, too, had seen the passing of its early patriots: The Honorable Thomas Hartley, the Honorable James Smith, Major John Clark, Colonel David Grier, and many others, whose courage and leadership had rallied the County to the cause of Liberty.

But the fears of the Constitutional Convention that the people of America might not be "up to" the responsibilities of self-government were never realized. Thomas Hartley, during the first of his twelve terms in the Congress of the United States, had written in 1784:

"It is a pity that the people at large are so unequal to their situation. In Republics every man ought to think. Time may put us right, but we are, at present, in the infancy of thought."

By 1826 that stage of infancy had passed. The history of the York County Court House, like the history of the country and of the world, "is but the biography of great men." The men who administered justice, practiced law and conducted public affairs within its precincts constitute a distinguished company.

Among the prominent men of law and letters associated with the Court House, to name only a few, were Charles Barnitz who served in both the State Senate and the United States House of Representatives, David Cassat, first president of the York Bank and of the York Water Company, Judge Daniel Durkee, and Prothonotary William Barber, one of the commissioners for the first bridge between Wrightsville and Columbia completed in 1814. Best known on the national scene, was Richard Rush who moved from Philadelphia to practice law in York in 1829. Rush had been Attorney-General of the United States in 1814, he served as acting Secretary of State, Minister to Great Britain and to France under President Monroe, and held the post of Secretary to the Treasury in the cabinet of John Quincey Adams.

All of these men were interested in higher education and followed the tradition of Hartley, Smith and Clark by serving as trustees for the York County Academy, founded in 1787. This institution's need for scholars, well versed in the classics, attracted many college and university graduates who, sometimes, used the teaching profession as a stepping stone to law. One such young Dartmouth graduate, who arrived in York in 1815, was

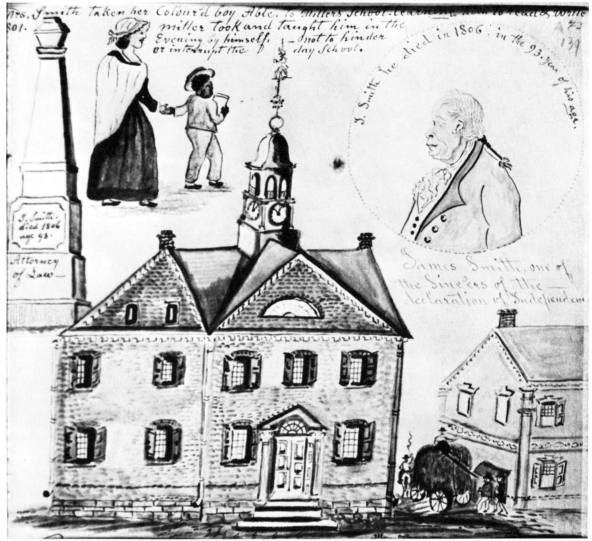

Lewis Miller drawing of Court House and the 1835 hay scale

Courtesy of Hist. Soc. of York Co.

Thaddeus Stevens. Although Stevens read law with David Cassat, a residency requirement prevented his admission to the York Bar. But while practicing in Gettysburg and Lancaster, he was a close associate of the York attorney, Edward Chapin, and a familiar figure at the York Court House.

Another New Englander to reach the Court House by way of the York County Academy was the amazingly brilliant and remarkably versatile Samuel Bacon. Highly successful as a teacher in Lancaster, he was invited to the Academy as an instructor in the classics shortly before the outbreak of the War of 1812. During the war he served as Quarter-master in the Marine corps and upon his return was admitted to the Bar. It was while practicing law in York that Bacon became interested in theology and the Sunday School movement.

York County Colonization Society

He tackled theology with his usual zeal, was ordained in Philadelphia as an Episcopal priest by the elderly Bishop White (former Chaplain to Congress) and almost immediately found a new challenge in the national movement for the Colonization of Free Persons of Color of the United States. This movement began shortly after the election of President Monroe, who advocated the colonization of freed slaves. In 1819 the United States government purchased a strip of the African coast to be known as Liberia — the capital — "Monrovia" — as the site of this experiment.

It was at the Court House on the evening of August 8, 1819, following a lecture on the subject, that the York County Colonization Society was organized in support of the national project.

When, on January 30, 1820, thirty families embarked for Liberia, Samuel Bacon was among them. But there was trouble from the beginning. His ship was delayed by ice, most of the passengers were seasick, there was a mutiny on board, the vessel leaked, and the prospective colonists became dissatisfied with the proposed distribution of land. The final tragedy was an outbreak of fever. The little colony was almost wiped out. One of the last victims was Samuel Bacon — May 12, 1820. His brief biography contributes a colorful footnote to the history of the Court House.

The influx of New Englanders into York County during the 1800's was not uncommon. Young America was on the move. Wheels were turning. There were new roads, new waterways, new opportunities. But as often happens in an era of growth, there was a certain amount of resistance to change. Regional pride and clannishness developed into prejudice and bigotry frequently expressed in caricatures, derogatory nicknames and epithets.

Petticoat Reporter

One of the most vocal bigots of this period was a notorious female journalist named Anne Royall, who used her privately owned press in Washington to attack everything and everybody of whom she disapproved. Missionaries in general, Presbyterians, Methodists, and Episcopalians in particular, as well as all New Englanders were among her most frequent targets. Anne Royall's visit to York in 1828 and her invasion of the Court House were the talk of the town!

Fortunately for Mr. McGrath his Globe Inn met with the visitor's approval and the distinguished company who crowded her parlor were also to her liking. But then, this sixty year old virago decided to visit the Court House . . . .

"Court was in session at the time, and who think you was the presiding judge? Even the wooden nutmeg man who traveled with me from Lancaster!"

This was Judge Bradford, a New Englander, of whom she had previously written:

"It is much to be lamented that these Pennsylvanians are not more particular in their choice of rulers, Having so much good sense and honesty among themselves, it is surprising they pick up those Yankee outlaws whom they exalt from selling tin buckets and horn flints to the Bench!"

No one who witnessed it would ever forget the scene that followed:

"His Honor had not taken his seat; and a number of good honest farmers being assembled in the court house, I made them a speech, which was received with great approbation. I told them of the danger of encouraging these blue-skin peddlers. They gazed at me in astonishment — it never came into their heads that Pennsylvanians would make as good judges as Yankees."

Time was when such an outburst would not have been tolerated, but times were changing. More people were "speaking out", and their language, especially their political language, was becoming increasingly disrespectful.

Era of the Common Man

No one would have dared refer to the first President of the United States as "Old Man Washington"! But the seventh president was "Old Hickory"! Former president, John Quincey Adams, became "Old Man Eloquent" during his subsequent career in Congress. The successful presidential candidate on the Whig ticket for 1840 was "Old Tip" or "Tippecanoe" Harrison.

This was the age of the political invective and the verbal brickbat. The common man was controlling the nation and as the issues became more critical, the political scene became more violent. Members of Congress shouted each other down with boos and bellows. Unpopular speakers were driven from public platforms under a barrage of rotten eggs and vegetables.

The York County Court House did not escape such scenes of disorder. On one occasion the appearance of the eccentric abolitionist, Jonathan

Blanchard, accompanied by Thaddeus Stevens, is reported to have "caused a great uproar" and was attended by "the throwing of missiles." On February 6, 1840 an abolition lecture by Charles E. Burleigh touched off a small riot.

Abolitionist Rallies and Riots

But in 1840, even in the excitement of an election year, the center of local interest was "The New Court House." In spite of the panic and depression of 1837, York had prospered, and the people demanded larger and grander accommodations for their county courts. They wanted a handsome new building, a real Temple of Justice, with spacious corridors and granite pillars, and they were, apparently, willing to spend nearly $100,000 to get it.

The New Court House

To the question — what to do with the old building — there was only one sensible, realistic answer, and this was a sensible, realistic age. The Court House was the property of the people. The people had built it, and now that it had become a useless eyesore and a barrier to progress, the people would tear it down.

And in September of 1841 they did just that. In spite of some idealistic opposition and a few sentimental protests, the proud little building was reduced to rubble. When the cupola was toppled, when the last wall was levelled, and the dust had settled, there was "a lonesome place against the sky."

The Sound of Silence

But this first York County Court House has been touched by immortality. "Domari Nolo!" It had not been subjugated by armies, it would not be vanquished by time! Its stones would not be silenced. They would speak to every generation. Through layers of cobblestones and cement, over the clatter of carriages, the clang of trolley cars and the roar of busses, would forever sound the echoes of greatness.

And in its new form, from its present location, the building that was the capitol and crucible of a new nation still speaks to every visitor and to every passerby. But it does not speak to all men in the same tongue or to the same purpose. Its message depends upon the ability to hear and understand.

Some, who pause and look up at the white cupola gleaming against the sky, may hear . . . nothing! Others may catch a dry whisper of dusty dates or half-forgotten facts. But those who open their hearts, will hear an affirmation of their faith in America and in themselves as worthy guardians of her destiny.

Bibliography

Bakeless, John, TURNCOATS, TRAITORS AND HEROES, Lippincott, New York, 1959

Boyd, Thomas, LIGHT — HORSE HARRY LEE, Charles Scribners, New York, 1931

Burnett, Edmond Cody (Editor) LETTERS OF MEMBERS OF THE CONTINENTAL CONGRESS., vols II and III. Carnegie Institution, Washington, 1921 — 1936

Carter, W. C., (and A. J. Glossbrenner), HISTORY OF YORK COUNTY FROM ITS ERECTION TO THE PRESENT TIME (1834), York, 1834

Duer, William Alexander, THE LIFE OF LORD STIRLING, Wiley and Putnam, New York, 1847

Dunlap, William, HISTORY OF THE NEW NETHERLANDS, vol. II, New York, 1840

Fletcher, Stevenson Whitcomb, PENNSYLVANIA AGRICULTURE AND COMMERCE, Pennsylvania Historical and Museun Commission, Harrisburg, 1950

Ford, Worthington Chauncey (Editor) JOURNALS OF THE CONTINENTAL CONGRESS, vols. IX, X, XI, Government Printing Office, Washington, 1908

Gibson, John (Editor) HISTORY OF YORK COUNTY PENNSYLVANIA, Chicago, 1886

Godcharles, Frederick A., DAILY STORIES OF PENNSYLVANIA, Milton, Pennsylvania, 1924

Graydon, Alexander, MEMOIRS OF A LIFE PASSED IN PENNSYLVANIA, John Wyeth, Harrisburg, 1811

Harley, Lewis R., LIFE OF CHARLES THOMSON, George W. Jacobs and Company, 1900

Hatch, Kohler, Terry, BICENTENNIAL ESSAYS ON YORK, PA, York, Pennsylvania, 1976

Heisey, John W., YORK COUNTY IN THE AMERICAN REVOLUTION, The Histroical Society of York County, 1971

Jensen, Merrill, THE ARTICLES OF CONFEDERATION, University of Wisconsin Press, 1940

Levy, Leonard W., FREEDOM OF SPEECH AND PRESS IN EARLY AMERICAN HISTORY, Harper and Row, 1963

Miller, Lewis, SKETCHES AND CHRONICLES, The Historical Society of York County, York, Pennsylvania, 1966

Mittelberger, Gottlieb, JOURNEY TO PENNSYLVANIA, Harvard University Press, Cambridge, 1960

Montross, Lynn, THE RELUCTANT REBELS, Harper and Brothers, New York, 1950

Morris, Richard B., THE PEACEMAKERS, Harper and Row, 1965

Morrison, Samuel Eliot, JOHN PAUL JONES, Little, Brown and Company, Boston, 1959

Prowell, George R., HISTORY OF YORK COUNTY, PENNSLYVANIA, Chicago, 1907

Rossman, Kenneth R., THOMAS MIFFLIN AND THE POLITICS OF THE AMERICAN REVOLUTION, University of North Carolina Press, 1952

Rupp, I. Daniel, HISTORY OF LANCASTER AND YORK COUNTIES, Lancaster, 1845

Scheer, George F. and Rankin, Hugh F., REBELS AND REDCOATS, World Publishing Company, 1957

Shephard, Jack, THE ADAMS CHRONICLES, Little Brown and Company, Boston, 1975

Smith, Ellen Hart, CHARLES CARROLL OF CARROLLTON, Harvard University Press, Cambridge, 1942

Spangler, Edward Webster, THE ANNALS OF THE FAMILIES OF CASPER, HENRY, BALTZER, AND GEORGE SPENGLER, York, 1896

Sparks, Jared, THE LIFE OF GOUVERNEUR MORRIS, vol. I, Gray and Bowen, Boston, 1832

Stroh, Oscar H., THOMPSON'S BATTALION, Paxton Herald, 1975

Swiggett, Howard, THE EXTRAORDINARY MR. MORRIS, Doubleday and Company, Inc., Garden City, 1952

Townsend, Sara, AN AMERICAN SOLDIER — THE LIFE OF JOHN LAURENS, Edwards and Broughton, 1958

Van Doren, Carl, SECRET HISTORY OF THE AMERICAN REVOLUTION, Viking Press, New York, 1941

Wallace, David Duncan, THE LIFE OF HENRY LAURENS, G. P. Putnam's Sons, New York and London, 1915

York County Records, Commissioners' Minute Books. Treasurers' Reports